Table of Contents

Unit 1   Language and Usage: The Sentence

1 What Is a Sentence?   1
2 Statements and Questions   3
3 Commands and Exclamations   5
4 The Subject of a Sentence   7
5 The Predicate of a Sentence   9
6 Correcting Run-on Sentences   11

Unit 2   Literature and Writing: A Story About Yourself

Writing a Good Beginning   13
Using Details   14
Writing a Good Title   15
Step 3: Revise   16
Step 4: Proofread   17

Unit 3   Language and Usage: Nouns

1 What Are Nouns?   19
2 Common and Proper Nouns   21
3 Nouns in the Subject   23
4 Singular and Plural Nouns   25
5 Plural Nouns with *es*   27
6 Plural Nouns with *ies*   28
7 Special Plural Nouns   29
8 Singular Possessive Nouns   31
9 Plural Possessive Nouns   33

Unit 4   Literature and Writing: Instructions

Topics and Main Ideas   35
Topic Sentences and Supporting
   Details   37
Purpose and Audience   39
Step 3: Revise   40
Step 4: Proofread   41

Unit 5   Language and Usage: Verbs

1 What Are Verbs?   43
2 Verbs in the Present   45
3 More Verbs in the Present   47
4 Verbs in the Past   49
5 More Verbs in the Past   51
6 The Special Verb *be*   53
7 Helping Verbs   55
8 Irregular Verbs   57
9 More Irregular Verbs   59
10 Contractions with *not*   61

Unit 6   Literature and Writing: Story

Beginning, Middle, and End   63
Writing a Good Ending   64
Characters and Setting   65
Step 3: Revise   66
Step 4: Proofread   67

D1736443

Unit 7 Language and Usage: Adjectives and Adverbs

1 What Are Adjectives?	69
2 More Adjectives	71
3 Using *a, an,* and *the*	73
4 Comparing with Adjectives	75
5 What Are Adverbs?	77
6 Other Kinds of Adverbs	79
7 Using *to, two,* and *too*	81

Unit 8 Literature and Writing: Description

Using Sense Words	83
Writing Topic Sentences and Choosing Details	84
Using Exact Words	86
Step 3: Revise	87
Step 4: Proofread	88

Unit 9 Mechanics: Capitalization and Punctuation

1 Correct Sentences	89
2 Capitalizing Proper Nouns	91
3 Capitalizing Other Proper Nouns	93
4 Abbreviations	95
5 Book Titles	97
6 Introductory Words	98
7 Commas in a Series	99
8 Quotation Marks	101
9 More About Quotation Marks	103

Unit 10 Literature and Writing: Letters

Writing Friendly Letters	105
Step 3: Revise	106
Step 4: Proofread	107

Unit 11 Language and Usage: Pronouns

1 Subject Pronouns	109
2 Pronouns and Verbs	111
3 Object Pronouns	113
4 Using *I* and *me*	115
5 Possessive Pronouns	117
6 Contractions	119
7 Using *there, their,* and *they're*	121

Unit 12 Literature and Writing: Research Report

Finding Information	123
Taking Notes	124
Writing a Paragraph from Notes	125
Step 3: Revise	127
Step 4: Proofread	128

Index

	129

LANGUAGE AND USAGE

1 | What Is a Sentence?

Sentences:	The very first cars looked strange.
	People laughed at them.
Not Sentences:	The very first cars.
	Laughed at them.

A. Read the two groups of words after each number. Underline the group of words that is a sentence.

1. The first automobiles amazed people.
   Rode on horses or bicycles.

2. A strange sight on the roads.
   Very few people had cars.

3. Inventors from different countries.
   Some cars had steam engines.

4. The Stanley twins built a steam car.
   The most famous of all the steam automobiles.

B. Write *sentence* if the group of words is a sentence. Write *not a sentence* if it is not a sentence.

5. Steam cars made so much noise.   _____

6. They were hard to start.   _____

7. Frightened horses.   _____

8. Accidents and angry words.   _____

9. Electric cars were quieter.   _____

10. Liked electric cars.   _____

11. Could not travel fast or far.   _____

12. Cars have changed since then.   _____

(continued)

LANGUAGE AND USAGE

1 | **What Is a Sentence?** *(continued from page 1)*

C. Writing Application: A Story

Pretend that you have invented an invisible car. Write a story that describes an adventure you had with this car. Write at least five sentences. Remember that each sentence must tell who or what and what happened.

Enrichment

Drive the car to the garage. Only take roads with groups of words that are sentences.

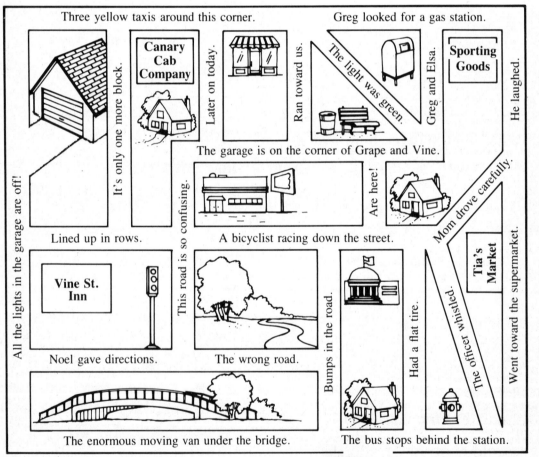

LANGUAGE AND USAGE

2 | Statements and Questions

> **Statement:** **O**ur country has a birthday.
> **Question:** **W**hat day is it on**?**

A. Write *statement* if the sentence tells something. Write *question* if the sentence asks something.

1. Another country ruled our land. _____

2. Many people wanted their freedom. _____

3. Was George Washington one of them? _____

4. Some men wrote an important paper. _____

5. What did that paper say? _____

6. Would our country become free? _____

B. Write each sentence correctly.

7. what month and day was that

_____

8. how old is our country now

_____

9. what happens every July 4

_____

10. people remember the birthday of our country

_____

11. there are big parades

_____

12. many people wave bright flags

_____

(continued)

Level 3 Unit 1 The Sentence   *(Use with pupil book pages 16–17.)*
Skill: Students will identify and will punctuate statements and questions.

C. Writing Application: A Letter

Imagine that you have been to a parade on our country's birthday. Write a letter to one of your friends. Write three statements that tell what you did and saw at the parade. Write three questions that you want to ask your friend.

Enrichment

1. The boy with the flag asks a question. Write the question.

_____

2. The girl wearing boots makes a statement. Write the statement.

_____

3. The girl with the drum asks a question. Write the question.

_____

4. The boy with the horn makes a statement. Write the statement.

_____

5. Does the man tell something or ask something?

_____

6. Write the sentence the man says.

_____

LANGUAGE AND USAGE

3 | **Commands and Exclamations**

> **Command:** **P**ull the fire alarm.
> **Exclamation:** **T**hat building is on fire!

A. Write *command* if the sentence tells someone to do something. Write *exclamation* if the sentence shows strong feeling.

1. Here come the fire engines! _____

2. Don't cross the street now. _____

3. Give them plenty of room. _____

4. The engines make so much noise! _____

5. The hook-and-ladder truck is huge! _____

6. Stay far away from the fire. _____

7. The smoke is so thick! _____

B. Write each sentence correctly. Use the clue in ( ).

8. thank goodness the fire is out **(exclamation)**

   _____

9. offer the firefighters a cool drink **(command)**

   _____

10. help them put away the hoses **(command)**

    _____

11. they look so tired **(exclamation)**

    _____

12. how brave they were **(exclamation)**

    _____

(continued)

LANGUAGE AND USAGE

3 | **Commands and Exclamations** *(continued from page 5)*

C. Writing Application: Instructions

Pretend that you are a fire chief. You want the engines, hoses, and ladders cleaned. Write three commands that you would put on the firehouse wall, telling the firefighters what to do. Then write three exclamations showing your excitement about the great job the firefighters did.

⭐ Enrichment ⭐

Rich wants to put out the campfire, but he doesn't know how. Write three commands to help him.

1. _____

2. _____

3. _____

Look at the picture. Find things that might make Rich feel excited, surprised, or afraid. Write three exclamations that Rich might say.

4. _____

5. _____

6. _____

LANGUAGE AND USAGE

4 The Subject of a Sentence

> subject
> **My friend** has a package of seeds.

A. Write each sentence. Then underline the subject.

1. Our class does an experiment for science.

   _____

2. We plant two bean seeds in different pots.

   _____

3. One pot gets no water.

   _____

4. Gary waters the other plant every day.

   _____

5. Leah checks the pot with the watered seed.

   _____

6. She sees a tiny bean plant.

   _____

7. Rico checks the unwatered pot.

   _____

8. He sees no plant at all.

   _____

9. Mrs. West explains the experiment.

   _____

10. Water helps seeds grow.

   _____

(continued)

LANGUAGE AND USAGE

4 | The Subject of a Sentence *(continued from page 7)*

B. Writing Application: A Science Report

Pretend that you are a scientist. You are doing an experiment to see if music helps plants grow. Write four sentences about your experiment. Give each sentence a different subject.

★ Enrichment ★

Count the flowers in front of each sentence. Write a subject with that number of words to complete the sentence.

1. _____ grows in a garden.

2. _____ do experiments.

3. _____
   _____ need more water.

4. _____
   _____ plant seeds.

5. _____
   _____ eat vegetables.

LANGUAGE AND USAGE

5 | The Predicate of a Sentence

subject   predicate
This book | **tells about jobs.**

A. Write each sentence. Then underline the predicate.

1. Many people work with animals.

   _____

2. Arlo works in a zoo.

   _____

3. He feeds the elephants every morning.

   _____

4. The monkeys play silly tricks on him.

   _____

5. The other workers laugh.

   _____

6. Maria is a special doctor.

   _____

7. She helps many animals.

   _____

8. Jeanette likes animals.

   _____

9. She owns a pet store.

   _____

10. All of her birds sing happily.

    _____

(continued)

LANGUAGE AND USAGE

5 | The Predicate of a Sentence   *(continued from page 9)*

B. Writing Application: A Journal

Pretend that you are an animal trainer for a circus. You train dogs, horses, and elephants to do all kinds of tricks. Write four sentences in your journal, describing what you taught the animals today. Use a different predicate in each sentence.

Enrichment

Underline the predicate of each sentence. Then write the first letter of the first word of each predicate. The letters will spell the name of the animal that each poem tells about.

1. This animal pushes over its feed pail.
   It is muddy from its head to its tail.
   It grunts happily from behind the wooden rail.   _____

2. It dives into the clear, cool pond.
   It uses its paddles very well.
   This bird crosses quickly to the shore beyond.
   It knows the sound of the farmer's dinner bell.   _____

3. A girl sees an animal.
   She hears a funny sound.
   This animal enjoys its dinner of grass.
   It eats everything on the ground.
   It plods lazily around and around.   _____

4. This tiny animal makes a noisy squeak.
   We open the barn door for a sneaky peak.
   The furry thing uses its sense of smell.
   It senses danger only too well.
   I enjoy this game of hide-and-seek.   _____

Level 3   Unit 1   **The Sentence**   *(Use with pupil book pages 22–23.)*
Skill: Students will identify and will write the predicates of sentences.

LANGUAGE AND USAGE

6 | Correcting Run-on Sentences

> **Wrong:** We use numbers every day they are everywhere.
> Numbers are helpful could we do without them?
>
> **Right:** We use numbers every day. **T**hey are everywhere.
> Numbers are helpful. **C**ould we do without them?

A. Correct each run-on sentence. Use capital letters and end marks correctly.

1. We like arithmetic numbers are fun.

   _____

2. Beth adds many numbers her answers are usually right.

   _____

3. Some problems are hard can anyone do these?

   _____

4. Hans divides quickly he finishes first in the class.

   _____

5. Jade uses numbers she counts her change.

   _____

B. Write *run-on* if the sentence is a run-on. Write *right* if the sentence is right. Fix each run-on sentence by adding capital letters and end marks.

6. Mario goes to a store he will buy food. _____

7. He buys two melons each melon costs a dollar. _____

8. He needs a pound of carrots. _____

9. Does he have enough money for the carrots? _____

10. Numbers are important we use numbers every day. _____

(continued)

6 | **Correcting Run-on Sentences** (continued from page 11)

C. Writing Application: A Math Problem

Pretend that you are a writer. You are writing a third grade math book. Write a word problem that is at least four sentences long. Be careful not to write any run-on sentences.

Enrichment

There is a secret message in these sentences. Find the run-on sentences, and fix them with a red pencil or marker. Write capital letters and end marks where they belong.

Today our class learned about shapes next week we will learn more. This shape has three sides it is called a triangle. What shape is this can you tell me? How many sides does a square have each square has four sides. Our teacher told us something what did she say? A circle is round other shapes are not round. What is a rectangle rectangles have four sides. We looked at pictures of kites kites have different shapes.

Write the red capital letters on the line. They spell a secret message for you.

Secret Message: _____

COMPOSITION SKILL: A STORY ABOUT YOURSELF

Writing a Good Beginning

Poor Beginning:	I stood on the sidewalk and looked up at the sky. All of a sudden, I noticed small pieces of paper falling. . . .
Good Beginning:	Was this really happening? Dollar bills were drifting down from the sky and covering the sidewalk. . . .

The following sentences come from different stories. The stories need beginnings. Read each story. Then write two good beginnings of one or two sentences for each story. Put a check next to the one you like better.

A. . . . I sat for a long time staring into the mirror. It was amazing how different I looked with a new haircut. The barber had just kept cutting and cutting. I looked like a round peach with a little fuzz on top.

1. _____

_____

2. _____

_____

B. . . . The old house was falling down on one side. Bats flew around the chimney. Jean and I walked softly up the front steps and looked through the window. A light flickered in the dark hall. We turned and ran down the flight of stairs. We didn't stop until we were all the way home.

1. _____

_____

2. _____

_____

Using Details

> Whenever you write, use enough details to paint a clear, lively picture for your reader.

A. Read each story. Put a check beside the one with details that paint a clear picture.

_____ Dad took us shopping. We went to the mall. We tried on a lot of shoes. I had a hard time choosing a pair. Finally, we both bought a new pair of shoes. Then we went home.

_____ Last Saturday afternoon, Dad took Karen and me shopping. The shoe store was very crowded. It was a long time before a clerk waited on us. Karen tried on at least a dozen pairs of shoes. She finally chose a pink pair with a blue stripe. I bought the first pair I saw. I wonder if Dad will ever take us shopping again.

B. Rewrite this story. Add enough details to help a reader picture what happens.

One Friday night Joe and I camped out at Boone River. We had a good time. The next day we went home.

_____

_____

_____

_____

_____

_____

_____

Writing a Good Title

Poor Title: The Day I Got Lost at the Supermarket
Better Title: Turn Left at the Fresh Fruit Counter!

Write two titles for each of the stories below. Put a check beside the one you like better.

A. _____

_____

The tree house was finished. Jesse and I hammered the last board into place. As we stood patting each other on the back, I realized that something was wrong. I checked the door, the window, the floor. Everything looked great. I looked up at the tree. Then I looked around me. ''Jesse,'' I muttered, ''why did we build this tree house on the ground?''

B. _____

_____

I wanted to surprise Mother. I had done the wash and was starting to fold the clothes. ''Where did all these pink clothes come from?'' I wondered. Then I knew. I had washed the white clothes with a red shirt. Mother would be having more surprises than I had planned today.

C. _____

_____

Mom and Dad had not been pleased with my last report card. The red letter beside the word *math* stood out like a sore thumb. I was determined to do better this month. Every night I studied my multiplication tables. Today I solved every example on the math test correctly. Now I might even join the superstars!

Step 3: Revise

Have I	yes
written a new beginning that will interest the reader?	☐
added details to paint a clear, lively picture?	☐
written a new title that fits and does not tell too much?	☐
changed stringy sentences to shorter sentences?	☐

Revise the following story. Use the check list above to help you. Check off each box when you have finished your revision.

● Use the space above each line, on the sides, and below the paragraph for your changes.

The Bike My Grandfather Gave Me

On Saturday the mail carrier delivered a box to my house. My name was on it, and no one knew what was inside. My mother helped me open the box. It seemed to take forever. I was so surprised I couldn't believe my eyes. Inside was a bicycle. It was from my grandfather and I called him right away to thank him and I was happy and I couldn't wait to show my new bike to my friends and so I rode it to the park.

Step 4: Proofread

which t̶e̶e̶m̶ would win this game/?
       ^team

Proofreading Marks	
⫪	Indent.
∧	Add something.
℈	Take out something.
≡	Capitalize.
/	Make a small letter.

Proofread the following story. There are four spelling mistakes and one run-on sentence. Three words should have capital letters. Two sentences have the wrong end marks. Use proofreading marks to correct the mistakes. Use a dictionary to check your spelling.

There is always a yard sale somewhere in my neighborhood.   My family had a sail last month.   I went threw my closet to find something i did not want anymore.   I chose my old roler skates I sold them to a girl who did not mind that one weel was missing.   she gave me a quarter.   Then what do you think happened this morning.   I opened my closet door and saw my skates. They were back. Was I seeing things. I was not.   It seems my brother had been to a yard sale.   he thought the skates were a good buy for thirty cents.

Name _____

LANGUAGE AND USAGE

1 | What Are Nouns?

> person   things   place
> My **uncle** has **cows** on his **farm**.

A. Write the two nouns in each sentence.

1. A farmer plants corn. _____

2. His daughter works in the field. _____

3. The tractor rolls over the ground. _____

4. The seeds go into the soil. _____

5. The girl walks down the rows. _____

6. Sun and rain are helpful. _____

7. Soon the plants are as tall as a person. _____

8. A big machine comes onto the land. _____

9. Many helpers pick the crops. _____

10. Workers load the heavy boxes. _____

11. Now the truck is full of vegetables. _____

12. The driver leaves the farm. _____

13. Some potatoes are sent to stores. _____

14. Carrots and peas go too. _____

15. People will buy the food. _____

B. Writing Application: A News Report

Pretend that you are a TV news reporter. A giant talking vegetable has just been discovered. Write a news report, describing the vegetable and where it was found. Use nouns that name people, places, and things.

(continued)

Level 3 Unit 3 Nouns   *(Use with pupil book pages 68–69.)*
Skill: Students will identify and will use nouns.

LANGUAGE AND USAGE

 1 | **What Are Nouns?**   (continued from page 19)

★ Enrichment ★

Write a noun to finish each rhyme. The rhymes tell about people, places, and things on a farm.

1. I am a person.
My name rhymes with *look*.
I make corn for dinner.
I am a _____ .

2. I am a place.
My name rhymes with *rake*.
People swim here.
I am a _____ .

3. I am a thing.
My name rhymes with *eat*.
I grow in the garden.
I am a _____ .

4. I am a place.
My name rhymes with *rest*.
A hen lays its eggs here.
I am a _____ .

5. We are people.
Our name rhymes with *ten*.
We are not women.
We are _____ .

6. I am a place.
My name rhymes with *hard*.
I have green grass.
I am a _____ .

7. I am a thing.
My name rhymes with *now*.
I give people milk.
I am a _____ .

8. I am a person.
My name rhymes with *fun*.
I am the farmer's child.
I am a _____ .

Now write two rhymes of your own on another piece of paper. Each rhyme should be about a noun that names a person, a place, or a thing. Draw a picture for each rhyme.

LANGUAGE AND USAGE

2 | Common and Proper Nouns

> common noun   common noun
> A **nurse** works at a **hospital.**
> proper noun   proper noun
> **Carol Pike** works at **Northside Hospital.**

A. Write *common noun* or *proper noun* for each underlined noun.

1. <u>Clara Barton</u> helped people all her life.   _____

2. She was a nurse during the <u>Civil War</u>.   _____

3. Miss Barton took care of many <u>soldiers</u>.   _____

4. She worked for the <u>Red Cross</u> in other lands.   _____

5. Clara began a Red Cross in the <u>United States</u>.   _____

6. The Red Cross can help people after a <u>storm</u>.   _____

B. Underline each noun. Write *CN* above each common noun and *PN* above each proper noun.

7. Little City had a bad flood last March.

8. Cars and trucks could not use the Rainbow Bridge.

9. On the radio, Mayor Mendez spoke calmly to the people.

10. Some children slept in the halls at the Holt School.

11. The Red Cross brought blankets and food.

12. By Friday the rain ended.

C. Writing Application: A Letter

Pretend that you work for the Red Cross. You are helping people who have left their homes because of a flood. Write a letter to a friend, describing your work. Include common and proper nouns.

(continued)

LANGUAGE AND USAGE

2 | Common and Proper Nouns *(continued from page 21)*

Enrichment

The picture below shows a part of Little City. Look at the numbered items in the picture. Then complete the chart below. Write a proper noun to match each common noun. The numbers on the drawing match the numbers on the chart.

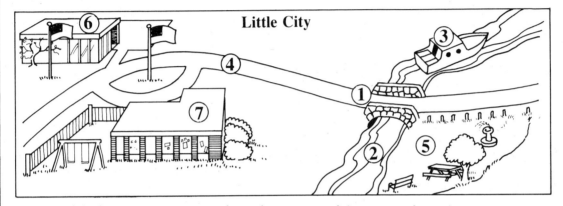

Little City

Now add three more people, places, or things to the picture. Number them *8, 9,* and *10* on the picture. Write a common noun and a proper noun to name each one.

COMMON NOUNS	PROPER NOUNS
1. bridge	1. Rainbow Bridge
2. river	2. _____
3. boat	3. _____
4. road	4. _____
5. park	5. _____
6. library	6. _____
7. school	7. _____
8. _____	8. _____
9. _____	9. _____
10. _____	10. _____

Level 3 Unit 3 Nouns *(Use with pupil book pages 70–71.)*
Skill: Students will write common and proper nouns.

LANGUAGE AND USAGE

3 | **Nouns in the Subject**

subject
Cold **weather** brings snow and ice.

subject
Ella Grotz loves winter storms.

A. Write the noun in the subject of each sentence.

1. A blizzard is not just snow. _____

2. Very strong winds blow in a blizzard. _____

3. Snow flies all around. _____

4. Tall trees bend in the wind. _____

5. Oaktown is having a blizzard. _____

6. Franklin Street is covered with snow. _____

7. Some cars are stuck on a hill. _____

8. All the squirrels hide in their nests. _____

9. Most people stay in their warm houses. _____

10. Ella Grotz puts on her boots. _____

11. Her heavy jacket will keep her warm. _____

12. The big plow is ready to go. _____

13. Mrs. Grotz drives the plow. _____

14. Al is her helper. _____

15. A yellow truck follows the plow. _____

16. Salt is put on the streets. _____

17. The ice melts into water. _____

18. A city needs good workers in a blizzard. _____

(continued)

LANGUAGE AND USAGE

3 | **Nouns in the Subject** *(continued from page 23)*

B. Writing Application: A Journal

Pretend that you have been snowed in by a blizzard. You have no electricity because of the storm. Write five sentences about this day. Underline the noun in the subject of each sentence.

★ Enrichment ★

Read each sentence below. Find and circle a noun in the puzzle to complete each sentence. Write the noun in the sentence. The words in the puzzle may run from left to right or from top to bottom.

S	R	J	A	C	K	N
L	N	A	F	H	I	F
E	S	N	O	W	B	R
D	T	U	V	K	O	O
S	H	A	T	S	O	S
C	A	R	R	O	T	T
B	O	Y	S	H	S	K

1. _____ is a winter month.

2. _____ makes everything white and sparkling.

3. Woolly _____ warm our heads in winter.

4. We left an orange _____ for the rabbit.

5. Many _____ and girls enjoy winter sports.

6. Shiny _____ line up for the race.

7. _____ keep our feet warm and dry.

8. _____ _____ visits only during winter.

Now choose four of the nouns that you circled. On another piece of paper, write four sentences, using each noun as the subject of a sentence.

LANGUAGE AND USAGE

4 | **Singular and Plural Nouns**

> **Singular Nouns:** We saw a **sparrow** in one **field**.
> **Plural Nouns:**   We saw many **sparrows** in those **fields**.

A. Write *singular* or *plural* for each underlined noun.

1. A sparrow is a small <u>bird</u>.   _____

2. Sparrows are found in many <u>states</u>.   _____

3. A sparrow makes its <u>nest</u> from grass and straw. _____

4. Sparrows also use <u>rags</u> in their nests.   _____

5. Soft <u>feathers</u> fill the bottom of the nest.   _____

6. A sparrow's <u>egg</u> is tiny.   _____

7. A <u>farmer</u> may not like sparrows.   _____

8. Sparrows often eat the <u>buds</u> of fruit trees.   _____

B. Choose the noun in ( ) that correctly completes the sentence. Write the sentence.

9. One kind of sparrow has a beautiful (song, songs).

   _____

10. Bird watchers often see these little (bird, birds).

   _____

11. Many (sparrow, sparrows) live in the city.

   _____

12. One sparrow has made a (home, homes) in our yard.

   _____

(continued)

4 | **Singular and Plural Nouns** *(continued from page 25)*

C. Writing Application: Directions

Imagine that you are a sparrow. Write directions to tell another sparrow how to find your nest. Describe trees, rocks, and other things to look for along the way. Use three singular nouns and three plural nouns in your directions.

Enrichment

Help the bird return to its nest. The bird can follow only paths that have plural nouns written on them. It must stay off all paths that have singular nouns.

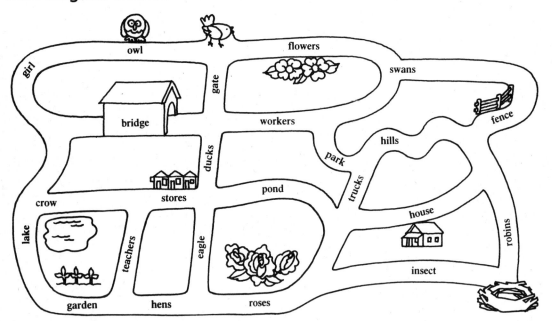

Now write four sentences describing the bird's trip. Underline each singular noun. Circle each plural noun.

_____

_____

_____

_____

LANGUAGE AND USAGE

5 | Plural Nouns with *es*

Singular Nouns:	circus	dish	branch	fox
Plural Nouns:	circus**es**	dish**es**	branch**es**	fox**es**

Write the plural form of the underlined noun to complete the second sentence in each pair.

1. Ms. Harris came with her <u>toolbox</u>.

   Other people brought _____ too.

2. Kira wanted to repair each <u>bench</u>.

   Everyone painted and repaired the _____ .

3. Marc forgot to clean his <u>brush</u>.

   All the other _____ were cleaned.

4. Each worker had a <u>glass</u> of milk.

   They put their empty _____ in the kitchen.

5. For the last project, they built a new <u>porch</u>.

   The Children's Center has two _____ now.

 # Enrichment

Write a one-word title for each picture. The title should be a plural noun.

1. _____   2. _____   3. _____

On another piece of paper, write one sentence about each picture. Include the plural noun you wrote below the picture. Then write a fourth sentence that uses all three plural nouns.

LANGUAGE AND USAGE

6 | Plural Nouns with *ies*

Singular Nouns	Plural Nouns
one **copy**	two **copies**
one **hobby**	many **hobbies**

Write the plural of the noun in ( ) to complete each sentence.

1. Edgar Allan Poe wrote poems and _____ . **(story)**

2. He often wrote _____ . **(mystery)**

3. Sometimes he wrote about _____ . **(family)**

4. Poe even wrote about their _____ . **(worry)**

5. He lived in New York and other _____ . **(city)**

6. Most _____ have books by Mr. Poe. **(library)**

★ Enrichment ★

Read the mystery riddle. The answer is written upside down.

Mystery Riddle: We are bigger than dimes.
We are worth less than nickels.
What are we?   pennies

Now write three mystery riddles of your own. Write the answer to each riddle upside down. The answer should be the plural form of a noun from the Word Box.

baby	butterfly	puppy	fly	diary	pony

_____

_____

_____

_____

Level 3 Unit 3 Nouns   *(Use with pupil book page 77.)*
Skill: Students will form the plural of nouns ending with a consonant and *y*.

LANGUAGE AND USAGE

7 | Special Plural Nouns

Singular	man	woman	child	mouse	tooth	foot	goose
Plural	men	women	children	mice	teeth	feet	geese

A. Use the plural form of the noun in ( ) to complete each sentence. Write the sentence correctly.

1. Many __?__ read fairy tales. (child)

   _____

2. In one tale, a cat wears boots on its __?__ . (foot)

   _____

3. Have you read about the cat with sharp __?__ ? (tooth)

   _____

4. Some furry __?__ wanted to put a bell on her. (mouse)

   _____

5. Did Mother Goose have one goose or many __?__ ? (goose)

   _____

6. Do men and __?__ really ride on birds? (woman)

   _____

7. I like the tale about the three giant __?__ . (man)

   _____

B. Writing Application: A Fairy Tale

Here is the first sentence of a fairy tale. ''Once upon a time, there was a frog with flat feet.'' Add five sentences to this fairy tale. Use the plural forms of four nouns from the Word Box.

child	man	goose	tooth	mouse	woman

(continued)

LANGUAGE AND USAGE

7 | **Special Plural Nouns** *(continued from page 29)*

Enrichment

Complete this crossword puzzle. Write singular and plural nouns to match the picture clues.

ACROSS

3.

7.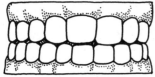

8.

9.

10.

DOWN

1.

2.

4.

5.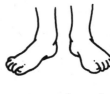

6.

Level 3 Unit 3 Nouns *(Use with pupil book pages 78–79.)*
Skill: Students will use singular and plural forms of irregular nouns correctly.

LANGUAGE AND USAGE

8 | Singular Possessive Nouns

Singular Nouns	Singular Possessive Nouns
horse	**horse's** owner
Janet	**Janet's** horse
cow	**cow's** ears

A. Write the possessive form of the noun in ( ) to complete the sentence.

1. _____ book has tall tales about Pecos Bill. **(Andy)**

2. Bill was wrapped in a _____ blanket. **(baby)**

3. The little _____ pet was a bear cub. **(boy)**

4. One day Pecos fell off his _____ wagon. **(father)**

5. He grew up in a _____ den. **(coyote)**

6. Later on, _____ horse threw him to the moon. **(Bill)**

B. Choose the correct noun from the Word Box for each sentence. Write the sentence correctly, using the possessive form of the noun.

cowhand	grandfather	wolf	Amy

7. Amy remembers her __?__ stories.

   _____

8. __?__ grandfather was a cowhand.

   _____

9. This __?__ life was never easy.

   _____

10. On many nights, a __?__ cry kept him awake.

    _____

(continued)

Level 3 Unit 3 Nouns *(Use with pupil book pages 80–81.)*
Skill: Students will form singular possessive nouns.

LANGUAGE AND USAGE

8 | Singular Possessive Nouns (continued from page 31)

C. Writing Application: A Diary

Imagine that you are a cowhand on a long cattle drive. You have ridden all day with the other cowhands. Write six sentences in your diary, describing your day. Use at least four singular possessive nouns in your sentences.

Enrichment

Draw a picture of a person or an animal from the Old West in each empty box below. Then draw something in the box that belongs to that person or animal.

1.

3.

2.

4.

Now write a sentence about each picture. Use a singular possessive noun in each sentence.

1. _____
2. _____
3. _____
4. _____

LANGUAGE AND USAGE

9 | Plural Possessive Nouns

Plural Nouns	Plural Possessive Nouns
brothers	**brothers'** boats
puppies	**puppies'** toys
walruses	**walruses'** teeth

A. Use the possessive form of the noun in ( ) to complete each sentence. Write the sentence correctly.

1. My __?__ boats are the *Hester* and the *Marie*. (**sons**)

   _____

2. Hester and Marie are my __?__ names. (**daughters**)

   _____

3. The girls work on their __?__ boat. (**cousins**)

   _____

4. The __?__ job is to pull in the nets. (**girls**)

   _____

5. They often hear the sea __?__ cries. (**birds**)

   _____

6. Many of our __?__ fishing boats are here too. (**friends**)

   _____

B. Writing Application: Sentences

Pretend that you sell fish in a big market. People also sell fresh fruit, vegetables, and other foods at this market. Write five sentences that describe the market and the good things people can buy there. Use a plural possessive noun in each sentence.

(continued)

LANGUAGE AND USAGE

9 | **Plural Possessive Nouns**   *(continued from page 33)*

★ Enrichment ★

Look at this silly picture.
Read the sentence about it.

Example: _The whales' pool_
is very cool.

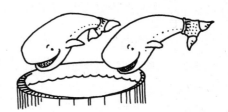

Now write a sentence about each silly picture below. Use a plural possessive noun in each sentence.

1. _____

   _____

4. _____

   _____

2. _____

5. _____

3. _____

6. _____

Level 3   Unit 3   Nouns   *(Use with pupil book pages 82–83.)*
Skill: Students will form and will use plural possessive nouns.

COMPOSITION SKILL: INSTRUCTIONS

Topics and Main Ideas

> The topic is the one thing that a paragraph is about. The main idea sums up what the paragraph tells about the topic.

A. Read each paragraph. Underline the answers to the questions.

Plant parts can be used to make dyes for yarn and cloth. Bark, roots, flowers, and berries are some plant parts used to make dyes. Cherries and beets make different red colors. Brown can be made from walnuts. Onion skins make a light yellow.

1. What is the topic?

   a. plants

   b. dyes

   c. cherries and beets

2. What is the main idea?

   a. how to make dyes from plants

   b. how to color cloth

   c. what the parts of a plant are

Do you know how plants get from one place to another? Seeds are scattered in several ways. The wind may blow seeds from one place to another. Seeds may be carried by water. Seeds can stick to an animal's fur. The animal may carry the seeds several miles before they drop off.

3. What is the topic?

   a. weather

   b. animals

   c. seeds

4. What is the main idea?

   a. how plants grow

   b. how seeds travel

   c. why an animal has fur

Can you tell the difference between a moth and a butterfly? The body of a moth is thick. A butterfly has a thin body. The feelers of moths are short and fuzzy. A butterfly's feelers are long, with little bulges on the end. Butterflies have colorful wings, but moths do not.

5. What is the topic?

   a. moths and butterflies

   b. parts of insects

   c. kinds of insects

6. What is the main idea?

   a. the body of a moth

   b. the body of a butterfly

   c. the difference between a moth and a butterfly

(continued)

COMPOSITION SKILL: INSTRUCTIONS

Topics and Main Ideas *(continued from page 35)*

B. Read each paragraph. Answer the questions.

1. Do you know how to turn a somersault? First, kneel on the floor. Put your hands on the floor in front of you. Then rest the top of your head on the floor between your hands. Finally, kick up both your legs and bring them all the way over your head.

    What is the topic? _____

    What is the main idea? _____

    _____

2. Ants eat different kinds of food. Some ants eat seeds. Other ants gather the juices from the flowers and stems of plants. Still other ants eat dead insects. One kind of ant eats mushrooms that grow on the pieces of leaf it brings into its nest.

    What is the topic? _____

    What is the main idea? _____

    _____

3. Did you think that spiders are insects? Well, they're not. Spiders are related to animals like crabs and lobsters. Spiders have eight legs. Insects have only six. The body of an insect is divided into three parts. The body of a spider has only two main parts.

    What is the topic? _____

    What is the main idea? _____

    _____

4. We know that Earth is shaped almost like a ball. We are sure because we have photographs. Astronauts have taken pictures in orbit and from the moon. Satellites have also sent back pictures that show our planet is ball-shaped.

    What is the topic? _____

    What is the main idea? _____

    _____

COMPOSITION SKILL: INSTRUCTIONS

Topic Sentences and Supporting Details

> The **topic sentence** states the main idea of a paragraph. The other sentences in the paragraph tell more about the main idea. They give **supporting details**.

A. Read each paragraph. Write the topic sentence of the paragraph.

1. You can make a mouse from a walnut shell. First, paint the walnut shell gray. Next, glue on black beads for the eyes and nose. Then cut the ears from black thread. Make whiskers from black thread. A piece of gray yarn makes a good tail.

    Topic Sentence: _____

    _____

    _____

2. An artist needs special materials to paint a water-color picture. Artists usually make water-color paintings on paper. First, they draw the picture with pencil or charcoal. Then they mix the water colors with water. They use several kinds of brushes to make the final painting.

    Topic Sentence: _____

    _____

    _____

3. Here are some tips for safe bicycling. First, make sure that your bike is in good working order. Check the brakes and test your lights and horn. Always obey all traffic signs and signals. Finally, never carry passengers on your seat or handlebars.

    Topic Sentence: _____

    _____

    _____

(continued)

COMPOSITION SKILL: INSTRUCTIONS

Topic Sentences and Supporting Details (continued from page 37)

B. Read each paragraph. A topic sentence is missing from each one. Decide what the main idea is. Write a good topic sentence.

1.   Pour about an inch of vinegar into a glass. Measure a teaspoon of salt and stir it into the vinegar. Place your dirty pennies in this mixture. Let the pennies soak overnight. In the morning, your pennies will be shiny and bright.

_____

_____

_____

2.   There can be a big difference in the price of a toy. Always check the price in several stores. Check newspaper ads for sales. Try to test the toy before you buy it. If the toy needs batteries, find out if they are included in the price.

_____

_____

_____

3.   You will need stage makeup in several bright colors. First, spread thick, white stage makeup all over your face. Next, paint your lips and your nose with red makeup. Then add blue eyebrows and other markings. Your clown face can be happy or sad. The bright colors will help people in the audience see your expression.

_____

_____

_____

Level 3   Unit 4   Instructions   (Use with pupil book pages 120–121.)
Skill: Students will write topic sentences.

COMPOSITION SKILL: INSTRUCTIONS

Purpose and Audience

> When you write, think of your **purpose**, or reason, for writing. Also think about your **audience**, or readers.

A. Read the sentences. Answer the questions.

1. You want to tell your friends how to find a book in the library.

   Who is your audience? _____

   What is your purpose? _____

   _____

2. You want to tell your brother how to fix a flat tire on a bicycle.

   Who is your audience? _____

   What is your purpose? _____

   _____

B. Kevin wrote two sets of instructions explaining how to get his baby brother ready for bed. Read the instructions. Then write *1* or *2* to answer each question.

1. Mom wants you to get Timmy ready for bed. Be sure to give him a bath and put a clean pair of pajamas on him. Then tuck him into bed and read him a story. When he falls asleep, turn off the light. Then tiptoe out of his room. You know what'll happen if he wakes up!

2. Tonight please get my little brother ready for bed. First, give him a bath and put pajamas on him. You'll find a clean pair in the top drawer. Then tuck him into bed and read him a story. He likes *Where the Wild Things Are*. When he falls asleep, tiptoe out of the room. Don't make any noise. If you do, he'll wake up and you'll have to read him another story.

   Which instructions did Kevin write for his sister? _____

   Which instructions did Kevin write for his friend? _____

Step 3: Revise

Have I	yes
written a topic sentence for the first paragraph?	☐
added order words and details to make the steps clear?	☐
put the steps in the correct order?	☐
replaced unclear words with exact nouns?	☐

Revise the following instructions. Use the check list above to help you. Check off each box when you have finished your revision.
● Use a thesaurus to help find exact words.
● Use the space above each line and on the sides for your changes.

A Game of Bottle Toss

You will need two half-gallon bottles with handles, paint, something to cut everything with, and foil. Cut the top half off the bottle, down from where you hold it. Leave some bottle below the handle. Do it again to the other bottle. Wad up the aluminum foil into a ball. Paint the tops. Make sure the ball fits.

To play, each person holds a bottle top with the cut end up. The ball is tossed back and forth from one to the other. You are ready to play bottle toss with someone. Both people try hard to make sure the ball does not fall.

THE WRITING PROCESS: INSTRUCTIONS

Step 4: Proofread

Bob's first ant farm was <u>very</u> ~~Not~~ ~~vary~~ successful?.

Proofreading Marks
⊓ Indent.
∧ Add something.
ꝰ Take out something.
≡ Capitalize.
/ Make a small letter.

Proofread the following instructions. There are three spelling mistakes. Two words need capital letters. One end mark is wrong and one is missing. Two apostrophes are missing, and there is a mistake in paragraph format. Use proofreading marks to correct the mistakes. Use a dictionary to check your spelling.

You have to be careful when you make a good ant farm. First, you need a large glass jar. take off the lid and punch holes in it with a hammer and a nail. Dig up a patch of dirt that has ants in it. Ants live in citys, so you should be able to get a lot. Fill the jar until it is about half full Put the lid back on. Finally, stuff little cotton balles into the holes in the lid. The cotton lets air into the jar but keeps the ants from getting out. Do not forget the ants food. every few days you should give them a few drops of water and some honey? Put the water in a dolls dish or in a bottle cap. Soon yor ants will start to feel right at home.

LANGUAGE AND USAGE

 What Are Verbs?

---

	verb			verb	
The eagle	**builds**	a nest.	The woman	**watched**	the eagle.
	predicate			predicate	

A. There is one verb in each sentence. Write the verb.

1. The eagle found twigs and branches. _____

2. It carried them to the top of a cliff. _____

3. It built its nest there. _____

4. It sat quietly in its nest. _____

5. Eagles catch small animals for food. _____

6. An eagle hunts for food every day. _____

7. The big bird flies high in the air. _____

8. Its sharp eyes see everything. _____

9. A small rabbit hops along. _____

10. The eagle spreads its huge wings. _____

11. It dives toward the rabbit. _____

12. The rabbit runs across the field. _____

13. It jumps quickly over a rock. _____

14. The rabbit hides safely in its hole. _____

15. The eagle returns to its nest. _____

16. It folds its strong wings. _____

17. The eagle closes its eyes. _____

18. It sleeps all through the night. _____

(continued)

1 | **What Are Verbs?** *(continued from page 43)*

B. Writing Application: A Report

Pretend that you are a scientist. You have been studying the strange and unusual yura bird. Write a report about the yura bird. Describe at least five different things that the bird does. Circle each verb.

★ ——— **Enrichment** ——— ★

Harry invented the machine in the picture below. Try to figure out how the machine works.

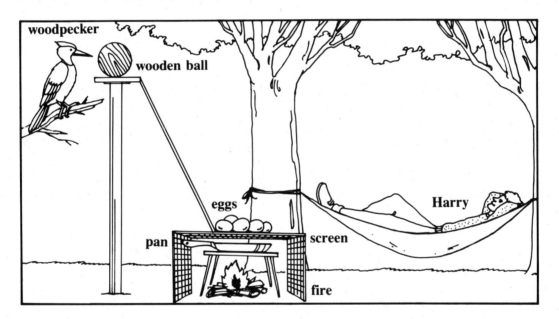

Write a verb to complete each sentence about the machine.

1. The woodpecker _____ the ball.

2. The ball _____ down.

3. The ball _____ the eggs.

4. The eggs _____ into the pan.

5. The fire _____ the eggs.

6. Harry _____ the eggs.

LANGUAGE AND USAGE

2 | Verbs in the Present

> **Singular Subject:** One <u>captain</u> **steers** the ship.
> **Plural Subject:** Two <u>captains</u> **steer** their ships.

A. Underline the correct present time verb in ( ). Then write each sentence correctly.

1. Workers (help, helps) us in many ways.

   _____

2. Mail carriers (bring, brings) our mail.

   _____

3. A doctor (keep, keeps) us healthy.

   _____

4. A librarian (choose, chooses) books.

   _____

5. An engineer (plan, plans) new machines.

   _____

6. Bus drivers (drive, drives) us to school.

   _____

7. Teachers (tell, tells) us about the world.

   _____

8. A baker (bake, bakes) bread.

   _____

9. Police officers (protect, protects) us.

   _____

10. An artist (make, makes) beautiful things.

    _____

(continued)

Level 3 Unit 5 Verbs *(Use with pupil book pages 140–141.)*
Skill: Students will choose present tense verbs to agree with singular and plural subjects.

LANGUAGE AND USAGE

2 | **Verbs in the Present** *(continued from page 45)*

B. Writing Application: A Letter

Pretend that you have a new job. Write a letter to a friend, describing your job and the people you work with. Use verbs in the present time. Underline the verbs.

Enrichment

Think of verbs that tell what the workers below are doing.

Describe what the workers are doing by completing the sentences below. Use a present time verb in each sentence.

1. Two workers _____ .

2. One man _____ .

3. Two women _____ .

4. A worker _____ .

Now draw two pictures of people working. Then write a sentence about each picture. Use a verb in the present time in each sentence.

5. _____

6. _____

Level 3 Unit 5 Verbs   *(Use with pupil book pages 140–141.)*
Skill: Students will use present tense verbs in sentences.

LANGUAGE AND USAGE

3 | More Verbs in the Present

Singular	Plural
One person **tosses** a ball.	Two people **toss** a ball.
One woman **washes** the car.	Two women **wash** the car.
One girl **catches** a bus.	Two girls **catch** a bus.
One man **fixes** the lamp.	Two men **fix** the lamps.
One boy **studies**.	Two boys **study**.

A. Underline the correct present time verb in ( ). Then write each sentence correctly.

1. Jet planes (fly, flies) across the ocean.

   _____

2. A plane (cross, crosses) the Atlantic Ocean.

   _____

3. The travelers (reach, reaches) the city of Paris, France.

   _____

4. People (rush, rushes) along the sidewalks.

   _____

5. A taxicab (splash, splashes) through puddles.

   _____

B. Write the correct present time of each verb in ( ).

6. Ray _____ across a wide street. (**dash**)

7. The boy _____ to a museum. (**hurry**)

8. One visitor _____ famous paintings. (**pass**)

9. A woman _____ paints. (**mix**)

10. A girl _____ the artist. (**watch**)

(continued)

Level 3 Unit 5 Verbs *(Use with pupil book pages 142–143.)*
Skill: Students will choose and will form present tense verbs to agree with singular and plural subjects.

C. Writing Application: Sentences

Imagine that you are visiting the only factory in the world that makes yeckles. As you walk through the yeckle factory, you watch very carefully to see what is happening. Now write five sentences that tell how yeckles are made. Use a present time form of each verb from the Word Box.

mix	press	brush	stretch	dry

Enrichment

Write a present time verb for each clue. Write one letter in each box or circle.

1. Opposite of pulls ◯ ☐ ☐ ☐ ☐ ☐

2. Walks in a parade ☐ ◯ ☐ ☐ ☐ ☐ ☐

3. Wipes the dishes ☐ ◯ ☐ ☐ ☐

4. Repairs ☐ ◯ ☐ ☐ ☐

5. Cleans her teeth ☐ ☐ ☐ ◯ ☐ ☐ ☐

Now answer the riddle by writing the circled letters on the line below. Capitalize the first letter.

What is the capital city of France?

_____

LANGUAGE AND USAGE

4 | Verbs in the Past

Present: The children **watch** the experiment.
The teachers **answer** questions.

Past: The children **watched** the experiment.
The teachers **answered** questions.

A. Write *present* if the underlined verb shows present time. Write *past* if the underlined verb shows past time.

1. Marta <u>pours</u> water into a pan. _____

2. Carlos <u>added</u> some salt. _____

3. Diane <u>mixed</u> the salt and water. _____

4. All the children <u>watch</u>. _____

5. The salt <u>disappeared</u> in the water. _____

6. The teacher <u>lights</u> the stove. _____

7. The teacher <u>heats</u> the water. _____

B. Write the past time of the verb in ( ) to complete each sentence.

8. Soon the water _____ to steam. **(turn)**

9. The steam _____ away. **(drift)**

10. The children _____ into the pan. **(look)**

11. Some salt _____ on the bottom. **(stay)**

12. Boris _____ it on a scale. **(check)**

13. It _____ the same as before. **(weigh)**

14. The children _____ . **(smile)**

15. They _____ questions about the experiment. **(ask)**

16. The teacher _____ them. **(answer)**

(continued)

Houghton Mifflin English 3
Copyright © Houghton Mifflin Company. All rights reserved.

Level 3 Unit 5 Verbs   *(Use with pupil book pages 144–145.)*
Skill: Students will identify present and past tense verbs and will form past tense verbs by adding *-ed*.

4 | Verbs in the Past   (continued from page 49)

C. Writing Application: A Journal

Pretend that you are a scientist. You have made a great new discovery. Write about it in your journal. Use the past time of each verb from the Word Box.

| discover | start | fill | want | learn |

★ Enrichment ★

The children in the third grade class did a science experiment. Write six sentences, telling what the children did. Use a different verb in the past time in each sentence. The words in the picture may help you.

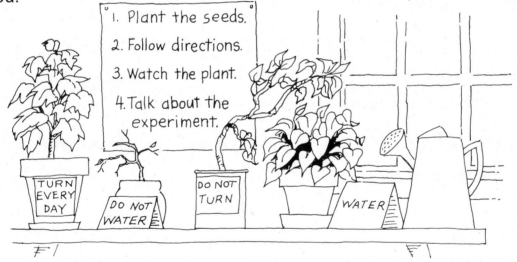

1. _____

2. _____

3. _____

4. _____

5. _____

6. _____

LANGUAGE AND USAGE

5 | More Verbs in the Past

> share + **-ed** = shar**ed**   cry + **-ed** = cr**ied**   sip + **-ed** = si**pped**

A. Write each sentence using the correct past time of each verb in ( ).

1. Our class __?__ the Aztecs. (**study**)

   _____

2. Long ago the Aztecs __?__ in Mexico. (**live**)

   _____

3. They __?__ corn and beans. (**raise**)

   _____

4. They __?__ food in the sun. (**dry**)

   _____

5. The Aztecs __?__ corn cakes over fires. (**bake**)

   _____

6. Our class __?__ an Aztec meal. (**plan**)

   _____

7. Greg __?__ the corn cakes flat. (**pat**)

   _____

8. Everyone __?__ a corn cake. (**try**)

   _____

B. Writing Application: A Magazine Article

Pretend that you are digging in Mexico. You discover some old pots, tools, and baskets. Write an article, telling how people used these things long ago. Use the past time of five verbs from the Word Box.

> use   dip   carry   bake   scrub   dance   chop

(continued)

Level 3   Unit 5   Verbs   *(Use with pupil book pages 146–147.)*
Skill: Students will form and will use the past tense of regular verbs that require spelling changes.

LANGUAGE AND USAGE

5 | **More Verbs in the Past**   (continued from page 51)

★ Enrichment ★

The Aztecs had no alphabet. They used picture writing instead. Picture writing works something like this. Each picture stands for a word. Together they form sentences.

farmer	rabbit	basket	carry	drop	hop	spy

race	pat	past time	a	the	into	away

Figure out the meaning of each picture sentence below. Write each sentence. Remember that the picture ← after a verb means that the verb is in past time.

1. • ⸾ ( ) ← • ⊖ _____

2. • ⸙ ∞ ← ˅ ⸾ _____

3. ˅ ⸾ ↓ ← ˅ ⊖ _____

4. ˅ ⸙ ⌢ ← ⌣ ˅⊖ _____

5. ˅ ⸾ ⊇ ← ˅ ⸙ _____

6. ˅ ⸙ ---- ← = _____

Now write your own picture sentences. You can use the pictures above or make up some of your own. Put the pictures together to make sentences. Then write the sentences in words.

7. [ ] _____

_____

8. [ ] _____

_____

Level 3 Unit 5 Verbs   (*Use with pupil book pages 146–147.*)
Skill: Students will use the past tense of regular verbs that require spelling changes.

LANGUAGE AND USAGE

6 | The Special Verb *be*

Present	**Past**
I **am** in a field.	I **was** here before.
Fong **is** my friend.	Lottie **was** with me.
We **are** outdoors.	They **were** busy.

A. Underline the correct verb in ( ) to complete each sentence.

1. I (am, are) curious about grasshoppers.
2. Grasshoppers (is, are) insects.
3. This grasshopper (am, is) green.
4. It (is, are) a good jumper.
5. Its hind legs (is, are) strong.
6. I (am, are) close to the grasshopper.
7. Walter (is, are) with me.
8. We (is, are) not afraid of the grasshopper.

B. Rewrite each sentence. Change each underlined verb to show past time.

9. Our play is about insects.

   _____

10. We are all in the play.

    _____

11. I am a grasshopper.

    _____

12. You are a butterfly. _____

13. Our friends are all there.

    _____

14. It is so much fun! _____

(continued)

Level 3 Unit 5 Verbs *(Use with pupil book pages 148–149.)*
Skill: Students will use present and past tense forms of the verb *be* to agree with singular and plural subjects.

LANGUAGE AND USAGE

6 | **The Special Verb be** (continued from page 53)

C. Writing Application: An Interview

Imagine that you are a grasshopper. A television reporter has come to ask you questions about your life now and your life as a baby grasshopper. Write the answers you will give. Use the verbs *am*, *is*, *are*, *was*, and *were*.

 Enrichment

Look at the pictures below. Write sentences to tell what the insects say.

1. The big grasshopper says a sentence with the verb *am*.

   _____

2. The small grasshopper says a sentence with the verb *are*.

   _____

3. The butterfly says a sentence with the verb *is*.

   _____

4. The ant says a sentence with the verb *were*.

   _____

5. The ladybug says a sentence with the verb *was*.

   _____

LANGUAGE AND USAGE

7 | Helping Verbs

Singular Subjects: Water **has** turned to ice.
She **has** learned about it.

Plural Subjects: Waves **have** splashed me.
We **have** watched the waves.

A. Write *has* or *have* to complete each sentence correctly.

1. We _____ learned much about the earth.

2. The earth _____ changed over many years.

3. Some islands _____ disappeared.

4. A new island _____ risen from the sea.

5. Whole forests _____ burned to the ground.

6. The rain _____ poured down.

7. It _____ washed soil away.

8. Streams _____ carried soil to new places.

9. The soil _____ become rich farmland.

10. Valleys _____ filled with water.

11. They _____ become new lakes.

12. This valley _____ become a river.

13. You _____ wondered what happens to mountains.

14. I _____ asked my teacher about this.

15. He _____ looked up the answer.

16. Some mountains _____ come from volcanoes.

17. Wind _____ worn down an old mountain.

18. This great mountain _____ turned into a hill.

(continued)

LANGUAGE AND USAGE

7 | **Helping Verbs** *(continued from page 55)*

B. Writing Application: A Story

Imagine that you are a very old mountain. You have been standing for many thousands of years. Write a story about your long life. Use the helping verb *has* or *have* in each sentence.

Enrichment

Help the Waverly family row down the winding river. Draw a route through places where the helping verbs *has* and *have* are used correctly. Then cross out each incorrect helping verb and write the correct verb above it.

They has called him.

Binky have tried hard.

They have entered the stream.

Binky have jumped in.

We has drifted off.

Ella has rowed.

They have continued.

You have followed us.

It has rained again.

I have rested.

The brothers have paddled.

I has fallen asleep.

We have explored.

Ray has rowed again.

Mother has shouted.

They has turned.

We have arrived.

The rain have stopped.

Dave have called us.

LANGUAGE AND USAGE

8 | Irregular Verbs

Present	Past	With *has, have,* or *had*
go	**went**	(has, have, had) **gone**
see	**saw**	(has, have, had) **seen**
do	**did**	(has, have, had) **done**
run	**ran**	(has, have, had) **run**
come	**came**	(has, have, had) **come**

A. Write the correct past time of the verb in ( ) to complete each sentence.

1. A ship had _____ to sea. **(go)**

2. I _____ on the ship as a sailor. **(go)**

3. Polly the Parrot had _____ with me. **(come)**

4. A sailor has _____ dark clouds. **(see)**

5. Rain has _____ down. **(come)**

6. High waves _____ onto the ship. **(come)**

7. We have _____ to the captain. **(run)**

8. Polly _____ into the cabin for safety. **(go)**

9. The sailors have _____ repairs. **(do)**

10. We _____ a good job. **(do)**

11. Then the captain _____ the sun. **(see)**

12. Polly _____ onto the deck again. **(run)**

B. Writing Application: A Ship's Log

Pretend that you are the captain of a ship. Each day you write in a big book called the ship's log. Write six sentences in the log about what has happened today. Use the past times of the verbs *go, see, do, run,* and *come.*

(continued)

Enrichment

Captain Sly gives Pedro Parrot a cracker each time he uses the right verb. Read the sentences that Pedro says. Write *cracker* beside the number of each sentence that has the right past time verb. Write the other sentences correctly.

1. The captain has saw a whale.

2. Many ships gone to the dock.

3. The sailors ran to the rail.

4. Waves have came onto the deck.

5. Captain Sly has done a good job.

6. The cook has ran to the kitchen.

1. _____

2. _____

3. _____

4. _____

5. _____

6. _____

How many crackers did Pedro Parrot get? _____

Now write another sentence for Pedro in the empty bubble. Use the correct past time of the verb *go, see,* or *run.*

9 │ More Irregular Verbs

Present	Past	With *has, have,* or *had*
give	**gave**	(has, have, had) **given**
write	**wrote**	(has, have, had) **written**
eat	**ate**	(has, have, had) **eaten**
take	**took**	(has, have, had) **taken**
grow	**grew**	(has, have, had) **grown**

A. Write the correct past time of the verb in ( ) to complete each sentence.

1. Rice has _____ us many new dishes to eat. **(give)**

2. People in many lands have _____ rice. **(eat)**

3. Rice probably _____ first in Asia. **(grow)**

4. Most of the world's rice has _____ in China. **(grow)**

5. Chinese people _____ many kinds of rice dishes. **(eat)**

6. Sailors had _____ rice to other countries. **(take)**

7. Farmers have _____ it in warm, wet places. **(grow)**

8. Traders _____ rice for other goods. **(give)**

9. Someone _____ about wild rice in America. **(write)**

10. Wild rice _____ in lakes in Wisconsin. **(grow)**

11. People _____ wild rice from lakes by canoe. **(take)**

12. Many people have _____ about rice. **(write)**

B. Writing Application: A Journal

Pretend that you are a trader long ago. You have traveled far and wide, buying and selling goods. Write at least six sentences in your journal. Describe the things you have traded, the places you have been, and the people you have met. Use the past times of the verbs *give, write, eat, take,* and *grow.*

(continued)

LANGUAGE AND USAGE

9 | **More Irregular Verbs** (continued from page 59)

Enrichment

Complete each sentence below with the correct past time of a verb from the Word Box. Then write the verbs in the puzzle.

ACROSS

2. I _____ my old sneakers to Jo.

3. Grandma has _____ a poem.

5. Meg had _____ the prize tomato.

7. We _____ rice yesterday.

8. Raccoons had _____ my lunch.

10. The twins have _____ an inch.

DOWN

1. The judge has _____ his answer.

3. Jen _____ her name on the list.

4. Our uncles have _____ us home.

5. Roses _____ here last year.

6. Al _____ his ticket to us.

9. We _____ our umbrellas with us.

| eat |
| take |
| give |
| write |
| grow |

LANGUAGE AND USAGE

10 | Contractions with *not*

Two Words	Contraction
She **was not** going along.	She **wasn't** going along.
The girls **did not** wait.	The girls **didn't** wait.

A. Write the contractions for the words in ( ).

1. They _____ believe that the Tower of Pisa leaned. **(could not)**

2. They _____ seen anything else like it. **(have not)**

3. The tower _____ stand straight. **(does not)**

4. It _____ fallen over. **(has not)**

5. They _____ understand how it stays up. **(cannot)**

6. The builders _____ plan it that way. **(did not)**

7. There _____ any other towers like it. **(are not)**

B. Write each sentence. Use two words in place of each contraction.

8. The tower isn't in the United States.

   _____

9. Tanya and Dawn hadn't seen it before.

   _____

10. They don't remember seeing pictures of it.

    _____

11. Tanya wouldn't stand near the tower.

    _____

12. They won't ever forget it!

    _____

(continued)

10 | Contractions with *not* *(continued from page 61)*

C. Writing Application: Directions

Pretend that you are a builder. You tell workers how to build new buildings. The workers are making some mistakes on your newest building. Write six directions telling the builders what is wrong. Use a contraction with *not* in each direction.

★ Enrichment ★

Write a contraction for each word or words. Write one letter or an apostrophe in each box or circle.

did not □ ○ □ □ □ □

will not □ □ □ □ ○

should not □ □ □ □ ○ □ □ □ □

were not □ □ □ ○ □ □ □

was not □ ○ □ □ □ □

cannot □ □ ○ □ □

has not □ □ ○ □ □ □

Now write the circled letters below to find the hidden sentence about a famous tower in Pisa, Italy. Begin the sentence with a

capital letter. _____

COMPOSITION SKILL: STORY

Beginning, Middle, and End

Every story has a beginning, middle, and end. The **beginning** tells who or what the story is about. The **middle** is the main part of the story. It tells what happens. The **end** tells how the happenings in the story work out.

Here are the beginning and the ending of a story. Write the plan for two different middles for the story. Put a check beside the one you like better.

Martha was so excited! She ate her breakfast as quickly as she could. Then she grabbed her sweater and dashed to the front door.

"Good-by, Mom," Martha called, as she skipped down the porch steps.

It was Saturday. Uncle Bert had given Martha five dollars. She knew exactly what she would do with it.

Middle 1: _____

_____

_____

_____

Middle 2: _____

_____

_____

_____

Uncle Bert placed his hand on Martha's shoulder. He looked at her with a warm smile.

"I'm proud of you, Martha," he said. "You have made your grandmother very happy."

Writing a Good Ending

> The ending is an important part of every story. A good ending makes the reader feel the story is finished in a way that makes sense.

Write the plan for two good endings for this story. Put a check beside the one you like better.

Jessie's vacation had been exciting, especially the last week of it. She was in the garden with her father. A huge, brightly colored balloon had landed in the field, but something looked strange. There seemed to be no one on board.

The balloon hadn't collapsed on landing. It bounced a few feet and then came back down. Jessie stared, caught her breath, and slowly, very slowly, walked toward it.

Ending 1: _____

_____

_____

_____

_____

_____

Ending 2: _____

_____

_____

_____

_____

_____

_____

COMPOSITION SKILL: STORY

Characters and Setting

> Every story has characters and a setting. The **characters** are the
> people and animals in a story. The **setting** tells where and
> when a story takes place.

Pretend that you want to write a story about two children who
have difficulty getting along with each other. When they are
together—in school, at home, or on the playing field—one always
tries to outdo the other. Write answers to the questions below to
describe the two characters and the setting of the story.

Character 1:

What is the name of the character? _____

How does the character look? _____

_____

How does the character act? _____

_____

Character 2:

What is the name of the character? _____

How does the character look? _____

_____

How does the character act? _____

_____

Setting:

When does the story take place? _____

_____

Where does the story take place? _____

_____

Step 3: Revise

Have I	yes
checked that the story has a beginning, a middle, and an end?	☐
added details to help describe the characters and the setting?	☐
rewritten the ending to finish the story in a way that makes sense?	☐
changed some verbs to more exact verbs?	☐

Revise the following story. Use the check list above to help you.
Check off each box when you have finished your revision.
● Use a thesaurus for help finding exact words.
● Use the space above each line and on the sides for your changes.

The Sad Tree

One day Tony went to the park. His footsteps made

noise on the leaves on the ground. He was under a tree.

"Oh, woe is me," a voice said. "All my leaves are

falling off." Tony looked up. The tree was trying to

put the leaves back on its branches. Tony tried to

comfort the tree. He told it that its leaves would all

come back in the spring.

"Oh, woe is me," said the tree. "I'll never be

beautiful again!" Tony went to the tree every day, but

the tree wouldn't cheer up.

Step 4: Proofread

the runners stands̶ at the starting line.

Proofreading Marks

廿 Indent.

∧ Add something.

ℐ Take out something.

≡ Capitalize.

/ Make a small letter.

Proofread the following story. There are three spelling mistakes, and two words need capital letters. Two end marks are wrong, and one is missing. One verb needs an ending. There is one error in paragraph format. Use proofreading marks to correct the mistakes. Use a dictionary to check your spelling.

Caesar lived in a swamp!   Because he was a crocodile, he thought he could do anything he wanted.   The other animals feared him.

one night he wached a big sliver ball floating on the water.   He tried to grab it but couldn't.   Every night Caesar look at the ball getting smaller and smaller?   Then it went away

"The silver ball is gone!" Caesar showted to his mother.

"That's just the moon," she said.   "It'll be back."

"Will you help me get it?" caesar asked.

"I can't," said his mother.   "There are some things even a crocodile can't have."

Name _____ WORKBOOK
PLUS ▲ 69

LANGUAGE AND USAGE

1 **What Are Adjectives?**

We like **quiet** music.   We heard a **large** band.

A. Write the adjective in each sentence.

1. Roberto and I went to a great concert. _____

2. People in the band wore black clothes. _____

3. The leader raised a short stick. _____

4. Beautiful music filled the room. _____

5. First, the band played a slow song. _____

6. They played a fast song after that. _____

7. A woman played a huge drum. _____

8. Loud sounds came from the drum. _____

B. Write each adjective and the noun that it describes.

9. People played small drums too. _____

10. Others played shiny horns. _____

11. I liked the silver flutes. _____

12. They play high notes. _____

13. Roberto liked the large instruments. _____

14. They make deep sounds. _____

15. The band played a sad song at the end. _____

C. Writing Application: A Review

Pretend that you write reviews for a newspaper. Write a review about a concert you have just heard. Use adjectives to describe the place, the music, and some of the instruments. Underline the adjectives.

(continued)

Level 3 Unit 7 Adjectives and Adverbs *(Use with pupil book pages 204–205.)*
Skill: Students will identify adjectives and the nouns that they modify.

Enrichment

Each instrument below is playing a song. The songs have some missing words. Use adjectives to complete each song.

Do you see the _____ band?

Listen to their _____ beat.

Clap your hands, stamp your feet,

Up and down the _____ street.

I met a _____ queen,

Driving a _____ car.

She sang a _____ song,

And wore a _____ star.

Now write your own song on the lines below. Be sure to use an adjective in each line of your song.

LANGUAGE AND USAGE

2 | More Adjectives

> Your body has **several** parts.
>
> **One** part of your body pumps blood.
>
> Your heart pumps blood through **many** tubes.

A. Write the adjective that tells *how many* in each sentence.

1. You have one heart in your body. _____

2. The heart pumps blood to many parts of the body. _____

3. It pumps five quarts of blood in a minute. _____

4. Two tubes go to the heart. _____

5. One tube brings blood into the heart. _____

6. Some blood is also carried away. _____

7. There are several doors inside the heart. _____

8. They let blood into the two sides of the heart. _____

9. Your heart beats about seventy times a minute. _____

10. Many hearts beat faster than this. _____

11. A few hearts beat more slowly. _____

12. An adult's heart is about five inches long. _____

13. It weighs about one pound. _____

14. Many animals have hearts too. _____

15. A few animals do not have hearts. _____

16. There are several ways to care for your heart. _____

17. One way is to eat well. _____

18. Getting some exercise helps your heart too. _____

(continued)

Level 3 Unit 7 Adjectives and Adverbs *(Use with pupil book pages 206–207.)*
Skill: Students will identify adjectives that tell *how many.*

LANGUAGE AND USAGE

2 | **More Adjectives**   (continued from page 71)

B. Writing Application: A Story

Pretend that you are a tiny creature. You live inside a heart. Write a short story about what it is like inside this heart. Tell what you hear, see, and feel. Use five adjectives that tell *how many*.

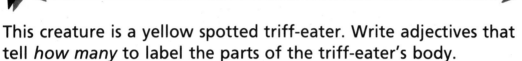

Enrichment

This creature is a yellow spotted triff-eater. Write adjectives that tell *how many* to label the parts of the triff-eater's body.

_____ wings   _____ feelers

_____ tail

                                                 _____ eyes

_____ legs

_____ spots

_____ toes on each foot

Now write four sentences about one day in the life of a triff-eater. Use adjectives from the Word Box in your sentences.

many	several	few	some

1. _____

2. _____

3. _____

4. _____

LANGUAGE AND USAGE

3 | Using *a*, *an*, and *the*

> One dinosaur had **a** long horn.
> That horn could scare away **an** enemy.
>
> **The** end of the horn was sharp.
> **The** dinosaurs ruled the land.

A. Write the correct article in ( ) to complete each sentence.

1. Mrs. Baker showed us _____ interesting picture. **(a, an)**

2. It showed _____ dinosaur. **(a, an)**

3. _____ dinosaurs were often very large. **(A, The)**

4. This dinosaur was much bigger than _____ elephant. **(a, an)**

5. It was much taller than _____ giraffe. **(a, an)**

6. _____ head was tiny. **(The, An)**

7. It had _____ flat beak. **(a, an)**

8. _____ smallest dinosaurs were the size of chickens. **(The, An)**

9. Dinosaurs lived _____ very long time ago. **(a, an)**

10. Some dinosaurs lived in _____ water. **(an, the)**

11. They ate _____ water plants. **(a, the)**

12. Some scientists found _____ egg from a dinosaur. **(a, an)**

13. _____ egg was six inches long. **(The, A)**

14. Others have found _____ bones of dinosaurs. **(a, the)**

15. We saw pictures of _____ enormous footprint. **(a, an)**

16. Three children were sitting inside _____ print. **(an, the)**

17. It was made by _____ big dinosaur foot! **(a, an)**

18. I can't imagine _____ animal that big! **(a, an)**

(continued)

Level 3 Unit 7 **Adjectives and Adverbs**   *(Use with pupil book pages 208–209.)*
Skill: Students will use articles correctly.

3 | Using *a*, *an*, and *the* (continued from page 73)

B. Writing Application: A Play

Pretend that you are a famous writer. You are writing a short play about two dinosaurs who meet at a small pond. Name each dinosaur and decide why they are at the pond. Write what each dinosaur says. Use the articles *a*, *an*, and *the* in your play.

★ Enrichment ★

Write a sentence to describe each dinosaur below. Use the article *a*, *an*, or *the* in each sentence.

1. _____
_____
_____

2. _____
_____
_____

3. _____
_____
_____

4. _____
_____
_____

LANGUAGE AND USAGE

 Comparing with Adjectives

> Maine is an **old** state.
> Ohio is an **older** state than Maine.
> New York is the **oldest** state of the three.

A. Choose the correct form of the adjective in ( ) to complete each sentence. Write the sentence.

1. Rhode Island is the (smaller, smallest) of all the states.

   _____

2. Texas is a (smaller, smallest) state than Alaska.

   _____

3. Arkansas has (warmer, warmest) winters than Alaska.

   _____

4. Florida has the (warmer, warmest) winters of the three.

   _____

B. Write the correct form of the adjective in ( ) to complete each sentence.

5. Colorado has _____ mountains than Maine. **(high)**

6. Alaska has the _____ mountain of any state. **(high)**

7. The _____ place in the United States is Death Valley. **(low)**

8. The East River is _____ than the Hudson. **(short)**

9. The Colorado River is the _____ of the three. **(long)**

10. Lake Huron is _____ than Lake Erie. **(deep)**

11. Lake Huron is _____ than Lake Superior. **(shallow)**

12. Lake Superior is the _____ of the Great Lakes. **(deep)**

(continued)

C. Writing Application: A Guidebook

Pretend that the new state of Squeakland has been added to the
United States. You are writing six sentences for Squeakland's
guidebook. Tell people why this state is special and what places they
should visit. Add *-er* or *-est* to some adjectives from the Word Box,
and use them in your sentences.

great	tall	new	old	warm	clean	fair

Enrichment

The map below shows the states of Ecks, Wye, and Zee.

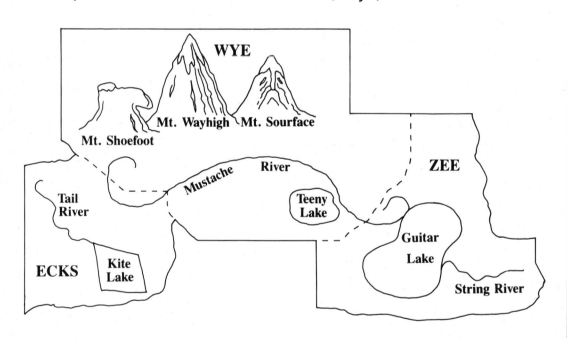

On another piece of paper, write six sentences, comparing the
places on the map. Use forms of the adjectives from the Word Box
in your sentences.

high	tall	big	small	short	long

LANGUAGE AND USAGE

5 | What Are Adverbs?

Swiftly the snow falls.

It flies through the air **quietly**.

The children **quickly** put on their boots.

The sun shines **brightly** on the snow.

A. Write the adverb that tells *how* in each sentence.

1. Snow lies thickly on the ground. _____

2. The teacher speaks cheerfully. _____

3. The children move swiftly. _____

4. They dress warmly. _____

5. Firmly they fasten boots and jackets. _____

6. They hurry happily out the door. _____

7. They quietly stand in a circle. _____

8. Carefully they pick up some snow. _____

9. They look at it closely. _____

10. A special glass helps them see it clearly. _____

11. They plainly see six sides on each snowflake. _____

12. The children politely take turns with the glass. _____

13. Rosa patiently waits for her turn. _____

14. She holds some snow tightly. _____

15. Eagerly she looks through the glass. _____

16. Suddenly she sees that the snow is gone. _____

17. It melted quickly! _____

18. Her friends gladly bring her more. _____

(continued)

Level 3 Unit 7 Adjectives and Adverbs   *(Use with pupil book pages 212–213.)*
Skill: Students will identify adverbs ending with *-ly*.

B. Writing Application: A Journal

Imagine that you are a snowflake. You have had a very exciting day. Write five sentences in your journal, telling about this exciting day. Use an adverb that tells *how* in each sentence.

Enrichment

Use adverbs that tell *how* to complete the crossword puzzle.

ACROSS
5. How you hold sharp things
6. How a lion roars
7. How you hold a kite string
9. How owls act in stories
10. How stars shine on cloudy nights

DOWN
1. How an unhappy person speaks
2. How you talk in a library
3. How your teacher wants you to write
4. How a turtle moves
8. How a truthful person speaks

LANGUAGE AND USAGE

6 | Other Kinds of Adverbs

> **When:** Nick **often** visits new places.
>
> **Where:** His family travels **far**.

A. Underline the adverb in each sentence. Then write *when* or *where* for each adverb.

1. Yesterday Nick visited an old village. _____

2. Nick's family lived nearby this village. _____

3. Early settlers built the village here. _____

4. Many settlers traveled far. _____

5. Today visitors explore the village. _____

6. Nick saw old houses there. _____

7. Someone had planted small gardens everywhere. _____

8. Women brought out gardening tools and baskets. _____

9. They always wear long dresses. _____

10. Nick visited an old kitchen first. _____

11. Next, he looked at the sawmill. _____

12. Big logs were piled around. _____

13. Later, he watched a horse pull a plow. _____

14. Nick will return often. _____

(continued)

Level 3 Unit 7 Adjectives and Adverbs   *(Use with pupil book pages 214–215.)*
Skill: Students will identify adverbs that tell *when* and *where*.

6 | **Other Kinds of Adverbs**   *(continued from page 79)*

B. Writing Application: A Report

Pretend that someone has invented a time machine. It can take you to the past or the future. Take a trip to another time. Write a report about the things you see and do. Use adverbs that tell *when* and *where*.

★ Enrichment ★

You have found a message written by someone long ago. The adverbs in the message are scrambled to keep them secret. Unscramble them to figure out the message.

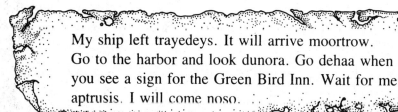

My ship left trayedeys. It will arrive moortrow.
Go to the harbor and look dunora. Go dehaa when
you see a sign for the Green Bird Inn. Wait for me
aptrusis. I will come noso.

1. When did the ship leave?   _____

2. When will it arrive?   _____

3. Where should you look?   _____

4. Where should you go when you see the sign?   _____

5. Where should you wait?   _____

6. When will the person come?   _____

Now pretend that you are living in the future. Write a secret message to arrange a meeting on another planet. Use at least five adverbs that tell *when* or *where*. Be sure to scramble the letters in the adverbs.

_____

_____

_____

_____

LANGUAGE AND USAGE

7 | Using *to, two,* and *too*

Words	Meanings	Examples
to	in the direction of	I go **to** the fair.
two	a number (2)	I went for **two** hours.
too	also	My friend went **too**.
	more than enough	Grandmother was **too** busy.

A. Write *to, two,* or *too* to complete each sentence.

1. Grandmother took her paints _____ the harbor.

2. She took her brushes _____ .

3. She painted for more than _____ hours.

4. Then it grew _____ dark for painting.

5. Grandmother carried everything back _____ the house.

6. She had painted _____ pictures of the harbor.

7. Grandmother and I took her paintings _____ the art fair.

8. Some paintings were _____ big for Grandmother's car.

9. She put a few paintings in her truck _____ .

10. I like the _____ paintings of the harbor.

11. Her other paintings are beautiful _____ .

12. Many people came _____ Grandmother's table.

13. There were _____ many people at one time.

14. One man bought _____ paintings.

15. A woman invited Grandmother _____ a big art show.

16. I hope that I can go _____ .

17. The show is _____ months from now.

18. The trip _____ the show will be fun.

(continued)

Level 3   Unit 7   Adjectives and Adverbs   *(Use with pupil book pages 216–217.)*
Skill: Students will use *to, two,* and *too* correctly.

LANGUAGE AND USAGE

7 | Using *to*, *two*, and *too* (continued from page 81)

B. Writing Application: An Article

Pretend that you write articles for an art magazine. You have been to an art show and have seen many different paintings. Write an article, telling which paintings you liked and which you didn't like. Explain your reasons. Use the word *to*, *two*, or *too* in each sentence.

Enrichment

Look at the drawing. Then write sentences about this picture. Follow the directions given below.

1. Write a sentence about the lobsters. Use the word *to*.

_____

2. Write a sentence about the seagulls. Use the word *two*.

_____

3. Write a sentence about the whales. Use the word *too*.

_____

4. Write a sentence, naming the drawing. Use *to*, *two*, or *too*.

_____

_____

COMPOSITION SKILL: DESCRIPTION

Using Sense Words

> **Sense words** tell how something looks, sounds, feels, smells, and tastes.
>
> A *strong*, *fishy* odor greeted the *scrawny* cat.

A. Read the following paragraph. Fill in each blank with a sense word that describes color, size, shape, sound, smell, touch, or taste. Then find and draw a line under six other sense words from the paragraph.

One day I watched a skinny, _____ beagle wander

down a _____ alley. Its coat was tangled and

_____ . Suddenly, I heard the _____

clanging of a lid hitting the _____ ground. All I could

see was a _____ tail hanging over the smooth sides of

the _____ garbage can. That old beagle was the only dog

I ever knew that liked the salty taste of _____ codfish!

B. Write at least four sense words to describe each item below.

1. a piece of chalk

_____

_____

2. a tree in autumn

_____

_____

3. a puddle

_____

_____

Name _____

COMPOSITION SKILL: DESCRIPTION

Writing Topic Sentences and Choosing Details

> When you write a description, begin with a topic sentence that states the main idea. Then choose details that support the main idea to create the picture you want.

A. Read each paragraph. Decide what the main idea of the paragraph is. Write a good topic sentence for each paragraph. Cross out the sentence that does not support the main idea.

1. The tiled floor was covered with sheets of used construction paper. Dirty brushes filled the sink. The sink itself had obviously not been cleaned for days. Some children had spilled jars of red and yellow poster paint on the table tops. I like working with poster paint. Paint dripped from the tables onto the floor.

   Topic Sentence: _____

   _____

2. A rumbling sound could be heard in the field near the farm. Many farmers raised corn and beans. At the edge of the field, smoke was pouring from an opening in the ground. Suddenly rivers of lava flowed from the crack. For days soot and ashes blackened the August sky. In a week's time, the volcano had reached a height of several hundred feet.

   Topic Sentence: _____

   _____

3. A waiter brought me a bowl of steaming noodles. I stared at the two thin wooden sticks that lay next to the bowl. Blue ceramic dishes were stacked on a shelf. There was no spoon or fork anywhere on the table. I picked up the chopsticks and tried to wind the noodles around them. Noodles have a mind of their own. They refused to give in to me. Instead, they slid back into the bowl.

   Topic Sentence: _____

   _____

(continued)

COMPOSITION SKILL: DESCRIPTION

Writing Topic Sentences and Choosing Details   *(continued from page 84)*

B. Read the topics in the box. Choose two of the topics. Write the name of each topic and five details to describe it. Then write a good topic sentence for each topic.

my bedroom	peanut butter
a rainstorm	my favorite shoes

Topic 1: _____

1. _____

2. _____

3. _____

4. _____

5. _____

Topic Sentence: _____

_____

_____

Topic 2: _____

1. _____

2. _____

3. _____

4. _____

5. _____

Topic Sentence: _____

_____

_____

Using Exact Words

> When you write a description, choose words that give a clear and exact picture.
>
> **Not Exact:** The animal was tired.
> **More Exact:** The little puppy lay sleepily on the rug.

A. Read each sentence below. Underline the word in ( ) that gives the clearer and more exact picture.

1. Luis (raced, went) across the field.
2. A (bird, robin) flew to the branch.
3. We grow (plants, pumpkins) in our back yard.
4. Two skaters (came, glided) over the ice.
5. My teacher (explained, said) why the sentence was true.
6. The wood had a (rotten, bad) smell.
7. A frog (sat, squatted) on the lily pad.
8. Hilda (stood, shivered) outside in the cold.
9. We sat watching a (fiery, nice) sunset.
10. Tony felt a (gentle, little) breeze on his face.

B. Read the words in the box and the following sentences. Fill in each blank with a word from the box that is more exact than the word in ( ).

screeched	pressed	deafening
rushed	shouted	giggled

11. I _____ the telephone close to my ear. **(put)**
12. "Come here quickly," _____ Kate. **(said)**
13. The cab _____ to a stop at the corner. **(came)**
14. I _____ inside the building. **(went)**
15. A _____ noise filled the hall. **(loud)**

Step 3: Revise

Have I	yes
added a topic sentence that clearly states the purpose of the description?	☐
replaced any details that do not support the topic sentence with details that do?	☐
used sense words to make the description clearer?	☐
used exact words to make the description clearer?	☐

Revise the following description. Use the check list above to help you. Check off each box when you have finished your revision.
● Use a thesaurus to help find exact words.
● Use the space above each line and on the sides for your changes.

My Stuffed Dog

Tuffy isn't very big at all. He is about as big as half a ruler. His hair used to be good, but it isn't anymore. It is sort of bumpy and worn because he is very old. He belonged to my mother when she was little. He is gray and has a white stomach. He has a nose that sticks out of his face. He has ears. He has a tail. One eye is a little bit dark, and the other one is white. He has a tongue that hangs from the side of his mouth. He makes a sound when I squeeze him. Some stuffed toys don't make any sounds. I like to hold Tuffy while I read. He is really lovable.

Step 4: Proofread

The air got ~~hoter~~ *hotter*. The sky grew ~~darkest~~ *darker*.

Proofreading Marks	
¶	Indent.
∧	Add something.
℘	Take out something.
≡	Capitalize.
/	Make a small letter.

Proofread the following description. There are three spelling mistakes, and two words need capital letters. Two end marks are wrong, and one is missing. There are two adjective mistakes. Use proofreading marks to correct the mistakes. Use a dictionary to check your spelling.

A badder dragon lived in a dark place. It was at the bottom of Mount zaramo. No one knows what this dragon was named, but it was very colorful. It had the bigest white teeth that anyone had ever seen. It had a bright gren tail that was longest than a train Even nicer than this were the dragon's two wings. these were a pretty purple and brown. If someone tried to go up to its cave, the dragon would make a loud noise. Smoke would come out of its mouth? If the person did not go away, the dragon would make a louder noise, and huge flames would come out of its mouth. Would you be scared of something like this. Only the braveest of knights dared to come near this dragon.

MECHANICS

1 | Correct Sentences

Statement:	Our country has had many Presidents.
Question:	Was Washington the first President?
Command:	Tell me the name of our sixth President.
Exclamation:	What a great President Lincoln was!

A. Write each sentence correctly.

1. our class is holding a contest

   _____

2. who can name all the Presidents

   _____

3. how can I learn all the Presidents' names

   _____

4. make a list of all the names

   _____

5. what a long list it is

   _____

6. our second President was John Adams

   _____

7. please tell me the name of the next President

   _____

8. what an easy question that is

   _____

(continued)

MECHANICS

1 | Correct Sentences   (continued from page 89)

B. Writing Application: A Letter

Write a letter to the President of the United States. Include statements, questions, polite commands, and exclamations in your letter. Begin each sentence with a capital letter and use correct end marks.

Enrichment

Pretend that you are touring a museum that has pictures of the Presidents of the United States. Look at the pictures of the first three Presidents. Then follow the directions below the pictures.

George Washington

John Adams

Thomas Jefferson

1. Write a statement about George Washington.

   _____

2. Write a question you would like to ask John Adams.

   _____

3. Write a polite command you would like to give Thomas Jefferson.

   _____

4. Write an exclamation about all three Presidents.

   _____

MECHANICS

2 | Capitalizing Proper Nouns

> Every **S**eptember, **A**unt **A**lba visits **M**ia **L**. **D**iaz and us.
> My aunt will take **F**ather and me to a parade on **S**aturday.
> She took her cat **P**irate to the parade on **L**abor **D**ay.

A. Write each sentence correctly.

1. Our city had a big parade for columbus day.

   _____

2. That was in the month of october.

   _____

3. Our friends lila m. swan and sonny selha led the parade.

   _____

4. The parade was on friday instead of saturday this year.

   _____

5. I saw uncle dave and my aunt riding on a float.

   _____

6. My uncle was dressed like christopher columbus.

   _____

7. I saw grandpa playing his tuba and grandma clapping.

   _____

8. My dog speedy watched the parade with mother and me.

   _____

(continued)

Level 3 Unit 9 Capitalization and Punctuation   *(Use with pupil book pages 266–267.)*
Skill: Students will identify and will capitalize proper nouns.

B. Writing Application: A Speech

Pretend that you are the mayor of a city. Your city has a special holiday to honor an important person in the city's history. Write a speech about this person and the new holiday. Use a proper noun in each sentence of your speech.

★ Enrichment ★

Read the letter below. Draw three lines under each letter that should be capitalized.

22 Cook Street
Elmhurst, IL 60126
January 16, 1990

Dear Janice,

Do you know olive p. norris? She gave a speech here one saturday last october or november. I went with ramona to hear her.

Guess what uncle ed gave me! His cat pepper had five kittens. Now I have a new kitten named rosebud!

Your friend,
Leah

Write the letters that should be capitalized. _____

Now unscramble the letters to spell two words that complete the sentence below.

Always capitalize _____ .

MECHANICS

3 | Capitalizing Other Proper Nouns

> Dela's grandparents live near **L**ake **C**hapala in **M**exico.
> They flew over the **G**ulf of **M**exico on their way to **C**hicago.

A. Write each sentence correctly.

1. Dela's grandparents visited the united states of america.

   _____

2. Dela lives near lake michigan in the state of illinois.

   _____

3. Her family went to the city of chicago for two days.

   _____

4. Her grandmother liked the flowers in lincoln park.

   _____

5. They all enjoyed the statues along dearborn street.

   _____

6. The tour of the university of illinois was fun.

   _____

7. They walked along michigan avenue to grant park.

   _____

8. Next week they will drive to the mississippi river.

   _____

B. Writing Application: A Travel Guide

Pretend that you are writing a travel guide for your own city or town. Tell visitors about interesting places such as lakes, parks, rivers, and schools. Underline the proper nouns.

(continued)

MECHANICS

3 Capitalizing Other Proper Nouns (continued from page 93)

★ Enrichment ★

You just moved to a town named Turtle Town. Turtle Town is unusual because each place is named for an animal. Write a name for each place shown on the map of Turtle Town below.

TURTLE TOWN

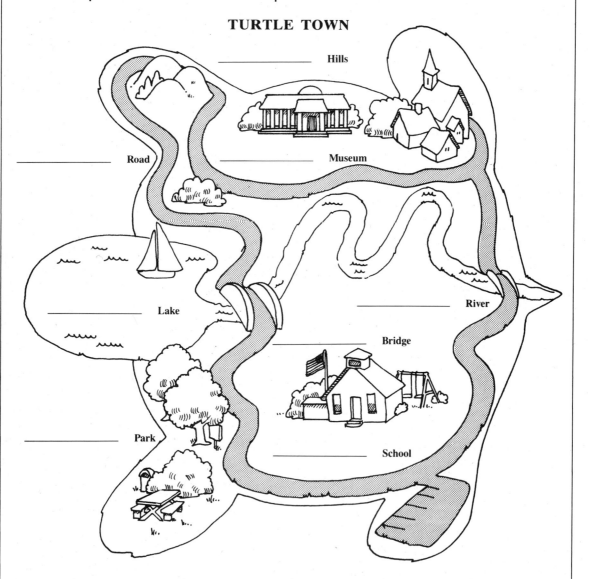

On another piece of paper, describe your first drive through Turtle Town. Write six sentences about the places you passed. Use a different proper noun in each sentence.

4 | Abbreviations

Days:	Tuesday	**Tues.**	Friday	**Fri.**
Months:	March	**Mar.**	October	**Oct.**
Titles:	Mister	**Mr.**	Doctor	**Dr.**

A. Write the correct abbreviation for each day and month.

1. Thursday _____   5. August _____

2. January _____   6. Wednesday _____

3. September _____   7. Sunday _____

4. Saturday _____   8. February _____

B. Write each title and name correctly.

9. mr frank chong _____

10. ms marisa alves _____

11. dr anita lynch _____

12. miss flo rivers _____

13. mrs sara varga _____

14. dr. bert king _____

C. Writing Application: A Journal

Pretend that you are traveling around the world. You travel by boat, by train, by bus, and on foot. Write a journal, telling about six days of your trip. Include each day's date and the names and titles of the people you meet along the way. Use abbreviations correctly.

(continued)

MECHANICS

 4 | **Abbreviations** *(continued from page 95)*

★ Enrichment ★

Pretend that you are a travel agent. You help customers plan their vacations. Read these notes about your customers' travel plans. Draw three lines under each letter that should be capitalized. Add periods where they are needed.

1. dr carol lamb leaves wednesday, january 1 returns saturday, february 1	**2.** mr mateo sanchez leaves saturday, march 22 returns sunday, may 4
3. ms mary kwan leaves tuesday, september 30 returns friday, october 28	**4.** miss gina rossi leaves monday, november 10 returns thursday, december 18

Now use the names and dates from the notes to fill in the travel schedule below. Use abbreviations for each title, day, and month.

	LEAVES		RETURNS	
Person	**Day**	**Month/ date**	**Day**	**Month/ date**
1.				
2.				
3.				
4.				

On another piece of paper, make a list of six special events for your class or a club that you belong to. Write the day and the month for each event. Use correct abbreviations.

Level 3 Unit 9 Capitalization and Punctuation   *(Use with pupil book pages 270–271.)*
Skill: Students will write abbreviations correctly.

MECHANICS

5 | **Book Titles**

Did Gipp like the book **A H**ot, **T**hirsty **D**ay?
Carla read poems from the book **T**he **H**ouse in the **W**oods.

Write each book title correctly.

1. sumi's prize _____

2. the birthday visitor _____

3. herman the helper _____

4. the star in the pail _____

5. a special trade _____

6. angus and the ducks _____

7. sunday for sonya _____

8. midnight on the mountain _____

Enrichment

Look at the book covers below. Make up a title for each book, and write it below its cover. Use underlining and capital letters correctly.

_____   _____

_____   _____

On another piece of paper, draw your own book cover. Write the title of the book on the cover.

MECHANICS

6 | Introductory Words

First**,** we got two bottles and some ice.
Then we started our experiment.
No**,** we didn't know what would happen.

Place commas where they are needed in these sentences.

1. Yes our class did a science experiment.
2. First we filled a bottle with very hot water.
3. Second we filled another bottle with cold water.
4. Next we poured most of the water out of both bottles.
5. Then we held some ice on the top of each bottle.
6. Well a cloud formed in one bottle.
7. Yes it was the bottle with the hot water in it.
8. No there was no cloud in the other bottle.
9. Then we talked about the experiment.
10. Finally we understood why the cloud had formed.

★ Enrichment ★

Look at the pictures below. Write a sentence about each picture to describe the experiment. Use *yes, no, well,* or an order word at the beginning of each sentence.

1. _____
2. _____
3. _____

MECHANICS

7 | Commons in a Series

Nancy, Felipe, and Dale learn about America.
They read, write, and draw in class.

A. Write each sentence correctly. Add commas where they are needed.

1. Canada Mexico and Peru are American countries.

   _____

2. Canada has mines for gold coal and iron.

   _____

3. People hike fish and camp in Canada's mountains.

   _____

4. Farmers in Canada grow wheat oats and potatoes.

   _____

5. Paper wood and oil come from Canada too.

   _____

6. Mexico has deserts mountains and jungles.

   _____

7. Oil iron and silver come from Mexico.

   _____

8. Farmers in Mexico grow sugar fruit and corn.

   _____

9. The Inca once lived worked and farmed in Peru.

   _____

10. Peru sells rice coffee and sugar.

   _____

(continued)

B. Writing Application: A Magazine Article

Pretend that you write articles for a magazine. Write five sentences for an article about the imaginary country of Thumpia. Describe the crops, jobs, and weather in Thumpia. Use a series of three or more words in each sentence.

Enrichment

Write six sentences about the picture below. In each sentence, use a series of three or more words.

1. _____

2. _____

3. _____

4. _____

5. _____

6. _____

MECHANICS

8 | Quotation Marks

> Bruno asked, "Why did people make arrowheads?"
> Jill replied, "They used them for hunting."

A. Write each sentence correctly. Add quotation marks where they are needed.

1. Jill said, Look at this old arrowhead.

_____

2. Jill added, It was made by people long ago.

_____

3. Bruno asked, What is it made of?

_____

4. Jill answered, This one is made of a stone called flint.

_____

5. Jill said, Arrowheads are made from other stones too.

_____

6. Bruno exclaimed, You know so much about arrowheads!

_____

7. Bruno asked, How did you learn about them?

_____

8. Jill answered, I read books about them.

_____

9. Jill added, I have seen arrowheads in museums too.

_____

10. Bruno said, I want to learn more about arrowheads.

_____

(continued)

MECHANICS

8 | **Quotation Marks** (continued from page 101)

B. Writing Application: An Interview

Pretend that you are a scientist. You have dug up many arrowheads, tools, and pots from long ago. A television reporter has come to ask questions about your discoveries. Write six sentences that you and the reporter might say to each other. Use quotation marks to show each person's exact words.

★ Enrichment ★

Each arrowhead has a scrambled word on it. Together these words will form a mystery sentence. First, unscramble each word.

 yaSmm

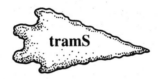 tramS

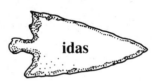 idas

1. _____   2. _____   3. _____

 hrworsAaed

4. _____

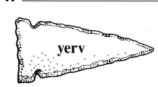 rea

 yerv

dlo

5. _____   6. _____   7. _____

Now complete the mystery sentence by writing the unscrambled words in the numbered spaces below. Add quotation marks to show the speaker's exact words.

_____ _____ _____ _____ ,
  1   2   3

_____ _____ _____ _____ .
  4   5   6   7

Level 3 Unit 9 **Capitalization and Punctuation**   (Use with pupil book pages 276–277.)
Skill: Students will write direct quotations correctly.

MECHANICS

9 | **More About Quotation Marks**

Dion said, **"M**y pencil is six inches long.**"**
Kari asked, **"D**id you measure it with this ruler**?"**

A. Write these sentences correctly. Add commas, capital letters, end marks, and quotation marks where they are needed.

1. Dion asked How many inches are in a foot?

_____

2. Kari answered, ''there are twelve inches in a foot''

_____

3. Luis added ''there are three feet in a yard.''

_____

4. Kari asked ''is a yard longer than a meter''

_____

5. Dion replied, A meter is a little longer than a yard

_____

6. Luis said, now let's measure the classroom.

_____

7. Dion said, we can use this yardstick.

_____

8. Luis exclaimed ''What a big job that will be''

_____

9. Kari said ''use the meterstick instead.''

_____

10. Luis shouted, This room is very long

_____

(continued)

Level 3 Unit 9 Capitalization and Punctuation   *(Use with pupil book pages 278–279.)*
Skill: Students will capitalize and will punctuate direct quotations.

B. Writing Application: A Conversation

Pretend that you and two friends are building a secret clubhouse. You have to measure, cut, and nail together some boards for the clubhouse walls. Write six sentences to show what you and your friends might say as you work. Use a quotation in each sentence.

★ Enrichment ★

Look at the picture below of Kate, Sherman, and Binh at their first club meeting. They are trying to decide which animal would make the best club pet.

Now imagine what Kate, Sherman, and Binh are saying about their pets. Write a quotation to complete each sentence below.

Kate asked _____

Sherman answered _____

Binh exclaimed _____

Sherman said _____

Kate added _____

Binh asked _____

Sherman replied _____

Kate exclaimed _____

Writing Friendly Letters

> A friendly letter has five parts. They are the **heading**, the **greeting**, the **body**, the **closing**, and the **signature**.

A. Tell what each part of a friendly letter does. Draw lines from the letter parts to what they do.

1. The **heading**   has a message.
2. The **greeting**   names the writer.
3. The **body**   says good-by.
4. The **closing**   names the person who gets the letter.
5. The **signature**   gives the writer's address and a date.

B. Read the following parts of a friendly letter. Then write the parts in the correct order.

Nicci

31 Mill Avenue
Dallas, TX 75208
May 16, 1990

Your niece,

Dear Aunt Carla,

Your visit next week will be wonderful. The weather should be nice, and the leaves will be colorful. I can't wait!

_____

_____

_____

_____

_____

_____

_____

Step 3: Revise

Have I	yes
used exact words in place of inexact words?	☐
added details to make the letter more interesting?	☐
added sentences that tell the reader I am thinking of him?	☐
put in order any parts of the letter that are out of order?	☐

Revise the following letter. Use the check list above to help you. Check off each box when you have finished your revision.
● Use a thesaurus to help find exact words.
● Use the space above each line, on the sides, and below the letter for your changes.

San Diego, CA 92131

15 Buena Vista Drive

June 6, 1990

Dear Grandpa,

My team won the championship. It was the last inning. My team was up. The score was tied. The bases were loaded. The player hit the ball. We won by four runs. I was the batter! I have some pictures of my team.

Love, Katie

Step 4: Proofread

Proofreading Marks
⊬ Indent.
∧ Add something.
℘ Take out something.
≡ Capitalize.
/ Make a small letter.

Please
~~Pleas~~ come to my ~~P~~arty. It's on friday at four o'clock.

Proofread this letter. There are two spelling mistakes. Five commas are missing. Two words should have capital letters. One end mark is wrong. Use proofreading marks to correct the errors. Use a dictionary to check your spelling.

44 Magnolia Street

Andalusia, AL 36420

August 28 1990

Dear Uncle reggie

    A man from the zoo came to scool yesterday. He brought a jiant parrot. It was red, green, yellow and blue. I asked the parrot if it wanted a cracker, and it answered me? Yes it really did talk.

        your nephew

        Lennie

LANGUAGE AND USAGE

1 | Subject Pronouns

Nouns	Subject Pronouns
<u>Charles</u> paints pictures.	**He** paints pictures.
<u>The pictures</u> are bright.	**They** are bright.

A. Write each sentence. Replace the underlined word or words with a subject pronoun.

1. <u>Charles and I</u> went to a museum in the city.

   _____

2. <u>The museum</u> had many paintings by Mary Cassatt.

   _____

3. <u>Mary Cassatt</u> was a famous American painter.

   _____

4. Did <u>Cassatt</u> live in France?

   _____

5. <u>France</u> has been the home of many artists over the years.

   _____

6. <u>Painters</u> have worked and shared ideas there.

   _____

7. <u>Charles</u> loves one of Cassatt's paintings called *The Bath*.

   _____

8. <u>This painting</u> is truly beautiful.

   _____

(continued)

Level 3 Unit 11 **Pronouns** *(Use with pupil book pages 326–327.)*
Skill: Students will use subject pronouns to replace nouns.

LANGUAGE AND USAGE

1 | **Subject Pronouns**   *(continued from page 109)*

B. Writing Application: A Description

Pretend that you and three friends are doing an art project in school. Write a short description of your project. Use at least five subject pronouns.

★ Enrichment ★

Charles painted a large picture showing what he thought things would look like in the future. Each small picture below is a part of his big painting. Write a sentence that describes each picture. Begin each sentence with a subject pronoun.

1.    _____

_____

_____

2.   _____

_____

_____

3.    _____

_____

_____

4.   _____

_____

On another piece of paper, draw your idea of a scene from the future. Write a description of your picture. Use subject pronouns in your sentences.

LANGUAGE AND USAGE

2 | Pronouns and Verbs

> She **takes** some special paper.   I **take** some special paper.
> It **matches** Mr. Ito's paper.   They **match** Mr. Ito's paper.
> He **makes** a bird.   We **make** a bird.

A. Write the correct verb form in ( ) to complete each sentence.

1. We _____ paper folding from Mr. Ito.   (**learn, learns**)

2. He _____ from the country of Japan.   (**come, comes**)

3. He _____ the art of paper folding to us.   (**teach, teaches**)

4. I _____ a bird with Lynda.   (**make, makes**)

5. She _____ the paper carefully.   (**fold, folds**)

6. I _____ the paper flat.   (**press, presses**)

7. She _____ up the folded paper.   (**open, opens**)

8. You _____ the bird's neck now.   (**see, sees**)

9. It _____ out so far!   (**stretch, stretches**)

10. She _____ the wings next.   (**make, makes**)

11. They _____ so beautiful.   (**look, looks**)

12. You _____ the bird up in the air.   (**hold, holds**)

13. It _____ ready to fly.   (**seem, seems**)

14. We _____ to Mr. Ito's stories of Japan.   (**listen, listens**)

15. They _____ many kinds of art there.   (**value, values**)

16. He _____ his friends in Japan.   (**miss, misses**)

17. They _____ to Mr. Ito often.   (**write, writes**)

18. I _____ to learn more from Mr. Ito.   (**hope, hopes**)

(continued)

LANGUAGE AND USAGE

2 | **Pronouns and Verbs** *(continued from page 111)*

B. Writing Application: A Story

Imagine that a paper bird meets two real birds. Write a short story to describe what happens. Use a subject pronoun and a present time verb in each sentence.

 Enrichment

Lynda made a puzzle from a paper circle. Find a verb from the Word Box to go with each subject pronoun in the outer circle. Write these verbs in the correct spaces of the inner circle.

trade
wishes
fixes
stop
climb
hides
cries
sit
jump

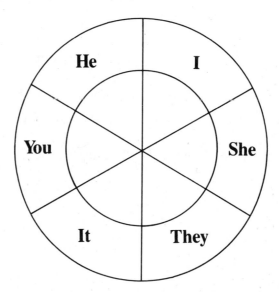

Now write sentences that begin with the pronouns and verbs that you matched in the puzzle. Add words to complete each sentence.

1. _____

2. _____

3. _____

4. _____

5. _____

6. _____

LANGUAGE AND USAGE

3 │ Object Pronouns

Nouns	**Object Pronouns**
I invited Judy.	I invited **her**.
Judy sat on a bench.	Judy sat on **it**.
Judy went with Mom and Bart.	Judy went with **them**.

A. Write each sentence. Use an object pronoun to take the place of the underlined word or words.

1. Mom took <u>Judy and me</u> to a hockey game.

   _____

2. We drove to <u>the sports center</u>.

   _____

3. The crowd cheered for <u>the players</u>.

   _____

4. The noise didn't bother <u>Judy</u> at all.

   _____

5. The goalie never let <u>the puck</u> into the net.

   _____

B. Write the correct pronoun in ( ) to complete each sentence.

6. One time the puck flew right at _____ . **(us, we)**

7. That scared _____ for a minute. **(me, I)**

8. Then the goalie waved at _____ . **(we, us)**

9. Judy waved back to _____ . **(he, him)**

10. We took _____ home after the game. **(her, she)**

11. Judy thanked _____ many times. **(us, we)**

12. She wants to come with _____ again. **(I, me)**

(continued)

LANGUAGE AND USAGE

3 | Object Pronouns (continued from page 113)

C. Writing Application: A Report

Pretend that you are a TV sports announcer. Choose a real or an imaginary sport. Write a report that tells your TV audience about the game you are watching. Use an object pronoun in each sentence.

Enrichment

Read these sentences about a hockey game. Put a check beside each sentence that has an object pronoun.

1. The coach watches us closely. _____
2. This big game is important to her. _____
3. The other team beat us last night. _____
4. They shot the puck across the ice. _____
5. The puck zipped toward me suddenly! _____
6. The goalie was ready for it. _____
7. Someone shot the puck at him quickly. _____
8. He blocked the play beautifully. _____
9. Noisy fans cheered for us! _____
10. We shouted with them. _____

Look at the sentences that have check marks. Write the underlined letters from these sentences on the hockey players' uniforms below. Write only one letter on each uniform.

Now unscramble the letters on the uniforms to find the secret word.

Secret Word: _____

LANGUAGE AND USAGE

4 | Using *I* and *me*

> I drink milk every day.   Milk is good for **me**.
> Ying and **I** are friends.   Ying visits Tom and **me**.

A. Choose the correct word or words in ( ) to complete each sentence. Write the sentence.

1. Ying showed (me and Tom, Tom and me) a milk carton.

   _____

2. (I, Me) saw the word *pasteurized* on the carton.

   _____

3. (Tom and me, Tom and I) wondered why.

   _____

4. Ying gave a book to (me and Tom, Tom and me).

   _____

5. (Tom and I, Tom and me) read about Louis Pasteur.

   _____

6. Ying told (I, me) that Pasteur was a great scientist.

   _____

7. (I and Tom, Tom and I) read that germs can grow in milk.

   _____

8. (Me, I) learned that Pasteur heated milk to kill germs.

   _____

9. Now milk is safe for (I, me) to drink.

   _____

10. Louis Pasteur's work has helped (Tom and me, Tom and I).

   _____

(continued)

LANGUAGE AND USAGE

4 | Using *I* and *me*   (continued from page 115)

B. Writing Application: A Report

Pretend that you are a scientist. You and your partner, Olga, have discovered a new way to keep food from spoiling. Write a short report that describes what you and Olga discovered and how you discovered it. Use *I* or *me* in each sentence.

Enrichment

Look at the picture below. Pete is teaching Eva and Mel how to make butter by hand.

Now read Mel's report about making butter. Mel has written the sentences in the wrong order. He has also made mistakes using the pronouns *I* and *me*. Write Mel's sentences correctly. Be sure to put them in the right order.

> Me and Eva found that the cream had turned to butter.
> Pete told Eva and I to pour the cream into the churn.
> Pete and me took the butter out of the churn.
> Pete wanted me and Eva to take turns beating the cream.

1. _____

2. _____

3. _____

4. _____

LANGUAGE AND USAGE

5 | Possessive Pronouns

Possessive Nouns	Possessive Pronouns
<u>Meg's</u> camera is small.	**Her** camera is small.
Meg went to <u>Jay's</u> party.	Meg went to **his** party.
Meg took the <u>guests'</u> pictures.	Meg took **their** pictures.

A. Write the possessive pronoun in each sentence.

1. Is that your new camera?   _____

2. It is different from my camera.   _____

3. George Eastman invented his new camera in 1888.   _____

4. Our cameras don't look like Eastman's cameras.   _____

5. Dorothea Lange is my favorite photographer.   _____

6. Many of her pictures are famous.   _____

B. Write each sentence. Use a possessive pronoun to take the place of the underlined word or words.

7. There are cameras in <u>Franco and Abe's</u> home.

   _____

8. Franco takes pictures of <u>Franco's</u> pet turtle.

   _____

9. Some pictures show the turtle in <u>the turtle's</u> shell.

   _____

10. <u>Millie's</u> favorite picture shows the turtle walking.

    _____

11. Abe takes pictures of <u>Abe's</u> pets too.

    _____

12. Abe also takes pictures of <u>Suzanne's</u> puppies.

    _____

(continued)

Level 3   Unit 11   Pronouns   *(Use with pupil book pages 334–335.)*
Skill: Students will identify possessive pronouns and will use them to replace possessive nouns.

LANGUAGE AND USAGE

5 | **Possessive Pronouns**   *(continued from page 117)*

C. Writing Application: Sentences

Pretend that you have a new camera. You have brought it to a birthday party in your class. Think of five pictures you might take at this party. Write a sentence to describe each one. Use a possessive pronoun in each sentence.

★ Enrichment ★

Write each group of words another way. Use a possessive pronoun.

1. the camera that belongs to me   _____

2. Jan's and Irv's smiles   _____

3. the camera's strap   _____

4. the film that belongs to you   _____

5. Leo's pictures   _____

6. Margaret's job   _____

7. photos that belong to Dad and me   _____

Look at the words you wrote in the answers above. Each word is hidden in the camera puzzle below. Circle these words. They are written across and down.

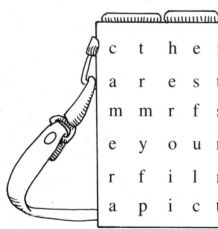

```
c t h e i r x m s t r a p
a r e s t s m i l e s n h
m m r f s         j u g o
e y o u r         o u r t
r f i l m       d b l x o
a p i c t u r e s r h i s
```

6 | Contractions

Two Words	Contraction
I have played computer games.	**I've** played computer games.
We will play one together.	**We'll** play one together.
You are winning!	**You're** winning!

A. Write the contractions for the underlined words.

1. We <u>have</u> talked about computers with Ms. Yee. _____

2. <u>She is</u> our math and science teacher. _____

3. <u>She has</u> shown us some new computer games. _____

4. I <u>will</u> tell you about one of them. _____

5. <u>It is</u> a game to practice math. _____

6. First, <u>you will</u> try to catch the frogs. _____

7. <u>They have</u> got numbers on them. _____

8. <u>I have</u> played this game at a friend's house. _____

B. Write the words that make up each contraction.

9. <u>We're</u> using this game in school. _____

10. <u>I'm</u> going to play it with Glenn. _____

11. <u>He's</u> played it before too. _____

12. He said <u>it's</u> helped him with math. _____

13. <u>He's</u> probably going to win this time. _____

14. Rob and Fran hope <u>they'll</u> play next. _____

15. <u>They're</u> excited about the new game. _____

16. <u>It'll</u> be fun for all of us. _____

17. <u>You've</u> wondered how to be better at math. _____

18. <u>I'm</u> sure this game can help you. _____

(continued)

LANGUAGE AND USAGE

6 | Contractions *(continued from page 119)*

C. Writing Application: An Advertisement

Pretend that you have invented a new computer game. Write an advertisement for this game. Describe how the game is played and why people should buy it. Use five contractions that are made with pronouns.

★ Enrichment ★

The computer screen below shows a game about contractions. Find the contraction in each sentence. Decide what letter or letters have been left out to make each contraction. Write the letters on the frogs.

1. _____ I'll play Funny Frogs with you.

2. _____ You're going to catch the frogs.

3. _____ I'm good at this game.

4. _____ It's fun to play.

5. _____ We'll have trouble catching those frogs.

6. _____ They're so fast!

7. _____ He's caught a frog.

8. _____ No, it's jumped away.

Now complete this secret sentence. Write the letters from the frogs in the correct spaces below. You will have to capitalize three letters.

_____ nk   _____ t   me   _____ nd   _____ .   _____ ll
  1   2   3   4   5

l _____ ugh.   _____ ,   _____ !
       6   7   8

LANGUAGE AND USAGE

7 | Using *there*, *their*, and *they're*

> We are going **there** to see Tony and Roma.
> We will go in **their** car.
> **They're** picking us up soon.

A. Write *there*, *their*, or *they're* to complete each sentence.

1. Tony and Roma invited us to _____ dance class.

2. We went _____ on Friday.

3. First, we met _____ dance teacher.

4. _____ very fond of her.

5. Chairs were _____ in the corner.

6. _____ for visitors to sit comfortably.

7. We sat _____ and watched.

8. Tony and Roma did _____ lessons well.

9. _____ very good dancers.

10. _____ big dance program will be held next week.

11. We're going _____ to see it.

12. _____ so excited about it.

13. They practice _____ dances every day.

14. I know _____ going to be the stars of the show.

B. Writing Application: An Invitation

Pretend that you are a dance teacher. You want to invite parents and friends to your students' dance program. Write an invitation to the program. Describe the dances that the students will perform. Use the words *there*, *their*, and *they're* in your invitation.

(continued)

LANGUAGE AND USAGE

7 | Using *there*, *their*, and *they're*   (continued from page 121)

★ Enrichment ★

The students in the dance class are practicing for a dance program. Look at the picture. Then write answers to the questions. Use the word *there*, *their*, or *they're* in each answer.

1. Who is teaching the dance class?

_____

2. Where are the children standing?

_____

3. What are the children wearing?

_____

4. Where is the dance class being taught?

_____

5. Where do the visitors sit?

_____

6. Are all of the children paying attention to the teacher?

_____

Level 3   Unit 11   Pronouns   *(Use with pupil book pages 338–339.)*
Skill: Students will use *there*, *their*, and *they're* correctly.

COMPOSITION SKILL: RESEARCH REPORT

Finding Information

> When you write a report, you can find some of the information you need in a dictionary, an encyclopedia, or an atlas, a book of maps.

Write *dictionary, encyclopedia,* or *atlas* to tell where you would look to find information about each topic.

1. Where is the Grand Canyon? _____

2. Who was Amelia Earhart? _____

3. How do you pronounce *safari*? _____

4. Who invented the first radio? _____

5. What does *portal* mean? _____

6. On what continent is Saudi Arabia? _____

7. What are the names of the Great Lakes? _____

8. What does *sullen* mean? _____

9. Why do fish have gills? _____

10. Into what gulf does the Red Sea flow? _____

11. When did Wisconsin become a state? _____

12. What does *excavate* mean? _____

13. Where was Thomas Edison born? _____

14. Where are the Marshall Islands? _____

15. Why do rainbows appear? _____

16. How long do redwood trees live? _____

17. How do you pronounce *decimal*? _____

18. What countries border Burma? _____

COMPOSITION SKILL: RESEARCH REPORT

Taking Notes

> When you take notes, write only enough words to help you remember the important facts.

Read each paragraph. Then take notes to answer the question that follows.

A.   Different trucks have different uses. Refrigerator trucks carry food that must be kept cold. Trailer trucks carry big loads over long distances. Tank trucks carry liquids. Vans carry furniture and other loads that must be protected from the weather. A dump truck has a bed that tilts so that the truck can unload things easily.

What are some of the uses of trucks?

_____

_____

_____

_____

_____

B.   The first trucks gave a bumpy ride. They were poorly made. Because the tires were made of solid rubber, the driver and load had a very uneven ride. Springs were also poorly made and did little to improve the ride. These trucks were very heavy. They often weighed more than the load that they carried.

Why did the first trucks give a bumpy ride?

_____

_____

_____

_____

_____

COMPOSITION SKILL: RESEARCH REPORT

Writing a Paragraph from Notes

> When you write a paragraph from your notes, use your question as the topic sentence for the paragraph. Make your notes the supporting details.

Write a paragraph from each set of notes. Use each question as a topic sentence. Write the notes as supporting details in complete sentences.

A. How long did children attend school in colonial days?
   —eight hours a day in summer
   —four hours a day in winter
   —two months in some towns
   —twelve months in other towns

_____

_____

_____

_____

_____

B. What was a schoolroom like in colonial days?
   —very bare
   —no chalkboards or chalk
   —few books
   —little heat
   —rows of hard benches

_____

_____

_____

_____

_____

(continued)

COMPOSITION SKILL: RESEARCH REPORT

Writing a Paragraph from Notes   *(continued from page 125)*

Write a paragraph from each set of notes below. Use the question as a topic sentence. Write the notes as complete sentences.

A. What was the furniture like in colonial homes?
   —thick wooden planks for tables
   —barrels, stools, and wood blocks for chairs
   —canvas bags stuffed with straw for mattresses
   —beds made of log slabs

_____

_____

_____

_____

_____

_____

B. What kinds of clothing did the colonists wear?
   —breeches and long linen shirts in summer for men
   —woolen breeches, knitted socks, and heavy shoes in winter
   —overcoats, leather leggings, woolen mittens, and fur caps
     outdoors
   —dresses of linen or wool for women
   —hooded capes outdoors

_____

_____

_____

_____

_____

_____

_____

Step 3: Revise

Have I	**yes**
used the question as the topic sentence of the paragraph?	☐
used in supporting sentences all of the facts from the notes?	☐
crossed out a sentence that gives an opinion?	☐
changed some pronouns to nouns to make the meaning clear?	☐

Revise the following paragraph from a research report. Use the check list above to help you. Check off each box when you have finished your revision.

● Use the space above each line and on the sides of the paragraph for your changes.

● Use the notes below to check that all the facts have been used in the paragraph.

How did the raccoon get its nickname?
—furry animal with black hair around eyes
—looks as if it is wearing mask
—nickname is masked bandit
—hunts at night
—steals food from garbage pails, chicken coops, houses
—strong, sharp claws can open doorknobs

The raccoon's nickname is the masked bandit. It is a

furry animal with black hair around its eyes. It looks

like a bandit's mask. It even acts like a bandit. It steals

food. Raccoons have strong, sharp claws. They can

even use them to turn a doorknob and enter a house. I

think that the raccoon's nickname is a good one!

Step 4: Proofread

Proofreading Marks	
⌐⌐	Indent.
∧	Add something.
ℒ	Take out something.
≡	Capitalize.
/	Make a small letter.

the girl ~~see~~ʲ *sees* the paper ~~mon~~ʲ *moon* and stars.

Proofread the following report. Find two spelling errors and two punctuation errors. Three words should have capital letters. There are two incorrect verbs and one mistake in paragraph format. Use proofreading marks to correct the errors. Use a dictionary to check your spelling.

Men's Shoes of the Past and present

During the Middle Ages, men wore an unusual style of shoe.   These shoes was made of soft leather, came in many colors, and had very pointed toes.   Sometimes the toes were stuffed to keep them stiff. This style was popular in Africa and the Middle East, but the fashion soon spred to europe.

Shoe styles have changed throughout history.   Today comfort is as important as fashion, Men wear work bewts and sport shoes because they lasts long and feel good.   these shoes don't crowd the toes like pointed shoes.   They often have rubber or leather parts Men wear them for walking, going to work, or for playing sports.

Index

a, an the, 173–74
Abbreviations, 95–96
Address, of a letter, 105
Adjectives, 69–76; articles, 73–74;
  comparative forms of, 75–76;
  identifying, 69–72; superlative
  forms of, 75–76
Adverbs, identifying, 77–80
Advertisement, writing activity for, 120
Agreement, pronoun and verb,
  111–112; subject-verb, 45–48,
  53–54
Apostrophes, in contractions, 61–62,
  119–120; in possessive nouns,
  31–34
Article, writing activities for, 51, 82,
  100
Articles, 73–74
Atlas, 123
Audience, for instructions, 39

be, forms of, 53–54
Beginnings, 63; revising, 16, 66;
  writing good, 13, 16, 66
Body, of a ltter, 105
Books, reference, 123; titles of, 97

Capitalization, of abbreviations, 95–96;
  of book titles, 97; proofreading for,
  17, 41, 67, 88, 107, 128; of proper
  nouns, 21–22, 91–94; of sentences,
  3–6, 89–90
Characters and setting, creating, 65;
  revising for, 66
Choosing details, 84–85
Closing, of a letter, 105
Commands, 5–6, 89–90
Commas, after introductory words, 98;
  with quotation marks, 103–104; in
  a series, 99–100
Common nouns, 21–22
Comparison, degrees of, 75–76
Composition skills, audience, 39;
  characters and setting, 65; exact
  words, 86, 87; finding information,
  123; note-taking, 124; parts of a
  letter, 105; proofreading, 17, 41,
  67, 88, 107, 128; purpose, 39;
  revising, 16, 40, 66, 87, 106, 127;
  supporting details, 37–38, 84–85,
  125–126; titles, 15; using details,
  14; using sense words, 83, 87;
  writing good beginnings, 13, 16,
  66; writing good endings, 64, 66;
  writing good middles, 63, 66;
  writing titles, 15, 16; writing topic
  sentences, 37–38, 40, 84–85, 87,
  125–126, 127
Contractions, 119–120; with *not,*
  61–62

Description, 83–88; proofreading, 88;
  revising, 87; using exact words, 86,
  87; using sense words, 83, 87;
  writing activity for, 110; writing
  topic sentences and choosing
  details, 84–85

Details, choosing, 84–85; revising, 16,
  40, 66, 87, 106; supporting, 37–38,
  84–85, 125–126; using, 14
Dialogue, punctuating, 101–104;
  writing activities for,102, 104
Diary, writing activity for, 32
Dictionary, 123
Directions, writing activity for, 26, 62

Encyclopedia, 123
End marks, 3–6, 89–90; exclamation
  points, 5–6, 89–90; periods, 3–6,
  89–90; proofreading for, 17, 41,
  67, 88, 107, 128; question marks,
  3–4, 89–90
Endings, 63; revising, 66; writing good,
  64, 66
Exact words, 86, 87; revising for, 40,
  66, 87, 106; using, 86
Exclamation points, 5–6, 89–90
Exclamations, 5–6, 89–90

Greeting, of a letter, 105

have, forms of, 55–56
Heading, of a letter, 105
Helping verbs, 55–56
Homophones, *there, their, they're,*
  121–122; *to, two, too,* 81–82

I, me, 115–116
Indenting paragraphs, proofreading,
  41, 67, 128
Information, finding, 123
Instructions, 35–41; audience for, 39;
  proofreading, 41; purpose of, 39;
  revising, 40; topic sentences and
  supporting details, 37–38; writing
  activity for, 6
Interview, writing activity for, 54, 102
Introductory words, 98
Invitations, writing activity for, 121
Irregular verbs, 57–60

Journal, writing activity for, 10, 24, 50,
  78, 95

Letters, 105–107; parts of, 105;
  proofreading, 107; revising, 106;
  writing activities for, 4, 21, 46, 90

Main idea, finding, 35–36, 84; revising
  for, 40

Narrative, personal,13–17
News report, writing activity for, 19
Notes, writing a paragraph from,
  125–126, 127
Note-taking, for reports, 124
Nouns, 19–34; common, 21–22;
  identifying, 19–20; plural, 25–30;
  plural possessive, 33–34; proper,
  21–22, 91–94; singular, 25–26;
  singular possessive, 31–32; in the
  subject, 23–24

Object pronouns, 113–114

Opinions, revising, 127
Order, revising, 40
Order words, 98; revising, 40

Paragraphs, identifying the main idea,
  35–36; indenting, 41, 67, 128;
  main idea, 35–36; proofreading,
  17, 41, 67, 88, 128; revising, 16,
  40, 87, 127; supporting details,
  37–38, 84–85, 125–126; taking
  notes for, 124; writing from notes,
  125–126, 127; writing a topic
  sentence for, 37–38, 84–85
Past tense, 49–52; of irregular verbs,
  57–60
Perfect tense of irregular verbs, 55–60
Periods, in abbreviations, 95–96; in
  sentences, 3–6, 89–90
Play, writing activity for, 74
Plural nouns, 25–30; irregular, 29–30
Plural possessive nouns, 33–34
Possessive nouns, 31–34; plural,
  33–34; singular, 31–32
Possessive pronouns, 117–18
Predicates, 9–10
Present tense, 45–48, 53–54;
  identifying, 49
Prewriting, identifying the audience,
  39; identifying the purpose, 39;
  note-taking, 124
Pronouns, 109–122; agreement with
  verbs, 111–112; contractions with
  119–120, *I, me,* 115–116; object,
  113–114; possessive, 117–118;
  revising, 127; subject, 109–110;
  there, their, and *they're,* 121–122
Proofreading, for capitalization, 17, 41,
  67, 88, 107, 128; descriptions, 88;
  for end marks, 17, 41, 67, 88, 107;
  instructions, 41; letters, 107; for
  punctuation, 17, 41, 67, 88, 107,
  128; research report, 128; for run-
  on sentences, 17; for spelling, 17,
  41, 67, 88, 107, 128; stories, 17, 67
Proper nouns, 21–22, 91–94
Punctuation, of abbreviations, 95–96;
  of introductory words, 98;
  proofreading for, 17, 41, 67, 88,
  107, 128; of quotations,101–104;
  of sentences, 3–6, 89–90; of titles,
  97
Punctuation marks, apostrophes,
  31–34, 61–62, 119–120; commas,
  98, 99–100, 103–104; exclamation
  points, 5–6, 89–90; periods, 3–6,
  89–90; question marks, 3–4,
  89–90; quotation marks, 101–104
Purpose in writing, instructions, 39

Question marks, 3–4, 89–90
Questions, 3–4, 89–90
Quotation marks, 101–104
Quotations, 101–104

Reference aids, 123
Research reports, 123–128; finding
  information, 123; note-taking, 124;
  proofreading, 128; revising, 127;

writing a paragraph from notes, 125–126, 127
Revising, beginnings, 16, 66; characters and setting, 66; descriptions, 87; details, 87; exact words, 40, 66, 87, 106; instructions, 40; letters, 106; research reports, 127; sense words, 87; stories, 16, 66; stringy sentences, 16; titles, 16; topic sentences, 40, 87, 127
Run-on sentences, 11–12; proofreading for, 17

Sense words, 83; revising for, 87
Sentences, 1–12, 89–90; capitalizing, 89–90; commands, 5–6, 89–90; exclamations, 5–6, 89–90; identifying, 1–2; predicates of, 9–10; punctuating, 3–6, 89–90; questions, 3–4, 89–90; revising stringy, 16; run-on, 11–12, 17; statements, 3–4, 89–90; subjects of, 7–8; topic, 37–38, 40, 84–85, 87, 125–126, 127; writing activities for, 33, 48, 118
Setting, creating, 65; revising for, 66
Signature, of a letter, 105
Singular nouns, 25–26
Singular possessive nouns, 31–32
Speech, writing activity for, 92
Spelling, contractions, 61–62; 119–120; forms of be, 53–54; irregular verbs, 57–60; plural nouns, 27–30; plural possessive nouns, 33–34; proofreading for, 17, 41, 67, 88, 107, 128; verbs in the past,

49–54; verbs in the present, 45–48
Statements, 3–4, 89–90
Story, 63–67; about yourself, 13–17; beginning, middle, and end, 63; characters and setting, 65; proofreading, 17, 67; revising, 16, 66; using details, 14; writing activities for, 2, 56, 72, 112; writing good beginnings, 13, 16, 66; writing good endings, 64, 66; writing good titles, 15
Story about yourself, 13–17; proofreading, 17; revising, 16; using details, 14; writing good beginnings, 13; writing good titles, 15
Stringy sentences, revising, 16
Study skills, taking notes, 124; using reference aids, 123
Subject pronouns, 109–110
Subjects, 7–8, agreement with verbs, 45–48; 53–54; finding nouns in, 23–24
Supporting details, 37–38; 84–85, 125–126

there, *their*, and *they're*, 121–122
Thinking skills, finding the main idea, 35–36
Titles, abbreviations of 95–96; of books, 97; capitalizing and underlining, 97; revising, 16
Topic sentences, 37–38, 40, 84–85, 125–126, 127

Usage, *a*, *an*, *the*, 73–74; *be*, 53–54;

comparing with adjectives, 75–76; helping verbs, 55–56; *I*, *me*, 115–116; irregular verbs, 57–60; object pronouns, 113–114; possessive pronouns, 117–118; pronouns and verbs, 111–112; run-on sentences, 11–12; subject-verb agreement, 45–48, 53–54; *there*, *their*, *they're*, 121–122; *to*, *two*, *too*, 81–82; verbs in the present, 45–48
Using sense words, 83, 87

Verb tenses, past, 49–52, 57, 59; perfect, 55–60; present, 45–48
Verbs, 43–60; agreement with subjects, 45–48; 53–54; helping, 55–56; identifying, 43–44; irregular, 57–60; past tense, 49–52, 57, 59; present tense, 45–48

Word choices, 86
Words, exact, 86, 87; introductory, 98; order, 98; sense, 83, 87
Writing applications, advertisement, 120; article, 51, 82, 100; conversation, 104; description, 110; diary, 32; fairy tale, 29; guide book, 76; instructions, 6; interview, 54, 102; invitation, 121; journal, 10, 24, 50, 78, 95; letter, 4, 21, 46, 90; math problem, 12; play, 74; report, 8, 44, 80, 114, 116; sentences, 33, 48, 118; ship's log, 57; speech, 92; story, 2, 56, 72, 112
Writing topic sentences and choosing details, 84–85